MW01013614

Nut Butter

OVER 50 CLEAN AND SIMPLE RECIPES TO FUEL A HEALTHY LIFESTYLE

Carolyn Cesario + Julie Sullivan
Cofounders of Ground Up Nut Butters

Andrews McMeel
PUBLISHING®

#spreadgood
#spreadgoo

Contents

GROUND
UP
GROUND
UP

CHAPTER 1:

Introduction

We are the "nut butter ladies," aka the cofounders of Ground Up, a small-batch nut butter company based in Portland, Oregon, that provides employment opportunity and job skills training to women overcoming adversity. We like to call ourselves a not-just-for-profit, meaning that we are most certainly a *for*-profit business but that we also exist to do more than make a profit; we aim to empower women.

Through the sale of healthy and delicious nut butters, we are able to hire and train women to work with us part-time as a means of getting back on their feet. We provide fair wages, mentorship, and training in all aspects of the business, from sales to production. We founded the company in 2016, and now, just a few years later, we are in over one hundred stores and employ eleven women. We'll get to more on our business model later. For now, we know you're really here for the nut butter.

All of our nut butters are made with clean ingredients. (No refined sugar or added oils.) We create them from unique blends of nuts, flavor them with natural spices, and use just a touch of honey for sweetness.

When selling our nut butters at markets and events, the question we most often get asked is, "So how do we actually use these?"

This cookbook is intended to serve as a comprehensive guide to assist you along your nut butter journey. If you're simply testing the waters, we've included a few easy recipes for adding our nut butters to your morning oatmeal or smoothie. If you're a seasoned vet, we'll show you how to incorporate nut butter into some wilder sauces (and even frost a cake with it!), and we'll also provide step-by-step instructions for making your own nut butter at home. In line with our own diets, we've tried to keep all recipes peanut-free, sugar-free, gluten-free, and dairy-free.

We hope this cookbook shows you that healthy and nourishing food can taste delicious, and that you leave wanting to incorporate more healthy fats into your diet. We hope that you get inspired by our flavor combinations and whip out your food processor to start a nutty kitchen party. And we hope that this cookbook provides fuel and nourishment for your adventures.

XO, CAROLYN + JULIE

Why Nut Butter?

The short answer: As active individuals, we've always enjoyed nut butters as healthy, quick fuel for our busy lifestyles. Making them is also incredibly fun; we love mixing up different flavors and combinations in our home food processors.

The long answer: Well, we'll let Carolyn share that.

CC: Cooking and preparing food has long been an important creative outlet for me. When I was working at a business consulting job that felt stifling to me, I would come home after long days at the office and turn my kitchen upside down. Tinkering with new, healthy recipes and blasting music took me to my happy place.

And, for whatever reason, my food processor has always been my favorite kitchen tool. I use it to make everything from homemade dips and sauces to granola bars—and, of course, nut butters. I think I'm drawn to the creative "mixology" involved in these types of recipes; adding "a bit of this" and "a dash of that" makes me feel inventive.

Five years ago, at age twenty-five, I was diagnosed with small intestinal bacterial overgrowth, more commonly known as SIBO. SIBO occurs when there is an overgrowth of bacteria in your small intestine, resulting in chronic pain. In my case, it meant over two years of brain fog, bloating, malnourishment, sleeplessness, muscle aches, and depression. At its simplest, it just felt like my body wasn't digesting anything properly.

Soon, cooking became a necessity, not just a creative outlet. I went on and off of various doctor-mandated diets, from GAPS to SCD to Low FODMAP. These are low-sugar, high-fat diets that restrict grain consumption, prohibit additives (so most store-bought food is excluded), and don't allow sugar (with the exception of small amounts of honey).

With all of the constraints, it was hard to buy anything at the grocery store, since most packaged foods contain additives and sugar. I would scour ingredient labels and special order items online, but for the most part, I had to cook my own food. (Which is quite a feat when you're working full-time!) On the plus side, I learned to do everything from making bone broth and fermenting yogurts to dehydrating apple chips.

As someone with a perpetual sweet tooth, the hardest part of these diets was not having chocolate or a proper dessert. So I began tinkering with my food processor in an effort to create delicious, creamy nut butters that both satisfied my sweet tooth and fit my diet. They were sweetened with just a touch of honey, free of peanuts and added oils, and used fresh vanilla bean and spices to create deep flavor profiles.

As many of Ground Up's loyal customers already know, fat-filled nut butters are an absolute treat—best enjoyed by the spoonful. When coworkers and friends tried my nut butters, they began asking for their own, so I started selling them as a side hustle, without the intention of doing anything more than sharing my creations with loved ones. I'm pretty sure I was actually losing money on this endeavor because nuts are pricey, and I thought it was a good idea to allow each person to customize their own flavor combination through an online form.

That's when I met Julie.

Business as a Tool for Social Good

Julie takes the story from here!

JS: When I met Carolyn, I had recently returned from Uganda, where I was managing an employment training program for 160 women on behalf of a jewelry company that helped women overcome poverty. After witnessing the success of this model of empowerment, I saw the opportunity (and need) to implement a similar training program in my hometown of Portland.

To better understand the issues women in our city were facing, I began interviewing various organizations and nonprofits. I quickly learned that part-time work for eight to twenty hours per week would be a huge help for many women trying to get back on their feet. I thought that if I could provide these women with an opportunity, along with basic job skills training and mentorship, they could gain the confidence and income they needed to transition toward stability and reach their goals.

After volunteering at nonprofits, where I got a better understanding of the frustrations of endless grant applications and oftentimes the disconnect between management and the people being served, I knew I wanted to start a for-profit business. Insert first roadblock: I didn't *have* a product to sell.

One of my early ideas was to run a custom sugar cube business. That didn't last long—on the way to my first sales meeting, I slammed on the car brakes and the sugar cubes crumbled to pieces. It's a good thing I met Carolyn when I did and didn't continue to pursue one of my many other, not-so-viable ideas.

While I have always loved nut butter as a fuel for my active lifestyle, I really got into "clean eating" out of necessity. When I moved home from Uganda, I was so excited to chow down on all of the foods I had missed. But, instead, I found that a lot of what I ate would make me feel sick. I was experiencing digestive issues, but I wasn't sure what was causing them. After living for two years on a diet consisting of what I could find at the local open-air market (primarily fruits, vegetables, and grains), my body was in shock from all of the processed foods.

I began to feel inspired to cook more; I wanted to understand what I was eating and where it came from and avoid unnecessary ingredients. In a way, I missed the many nights in Uganda cooking over an open charcoal fire, getting creative with the fresh ingredients we had on hand.

I've always enjoyed being active. Running, in particular, has been an outlet for stress relief and for calming my mind, but I began experiencing serious stomach cramping every time I ran. I felt trapped and at the mercy of my body's response to things. But the one thing I could control was my diet. I eliminated refined sugars, cut back on gluten, and discovered that I had an intolerance to dairy (goodbye, pizza or my morning yogurt that I loved). Nut butter and fruit became my go-to breakfast and snack.

When I met Carolyn and shortly thereafter tried her nut butters, I insisted on learning how to make them. (I promise I wasn't scheming to rope her into the business at that moment but instead thought it'd be fun to know how to make them on my own!) So I went to Carolyn's, and we spent the evening making nut butters, having a blast.

Carolyn asked me more about my vision for my training program and why I hadn't started it yet. I shared with her that I had been struggling to find a product, while Carolyn shared that she had always dreamed of starting a food company but felt that she didn't want to start a company without a larger purpose or mission. Plus, she told me, the nut butter category was already so competitive.

Now, we honestly can't recall who first suggested that we combine visions, but by the end of that night, it was clear that nut butters would be the product to bring this employment training program to life. (Or at least, what did we have to lose by trying?)

It also was clear that we would be moving on this idea *fast*. It was April 2016, and as two type-A overachievers, we set a goal to be selling our nut butters at all Portland-area farmers' markets by the summer. What we didn't know then is that we needed to sign up for these markets by December of the previous year . . . so while we may not have hit that goal, we did hit the ground running. We spent countless nights making nut butters in Carolyn's small kitchen, perfecting our recipes. There was a constant rotation of nuts toasting in the oven and the steady whirring of small, household food processors.

By the end of our first summer, we'd moved into a commercial kitchen space; and by the holidays of that year, we'd brought on our first intern (who is still with us—she has moved up to become our fulfillment lead).

Our Mission

We told you we'd circle back to this! Ground Up is a social enterprise that provides women overcoming adversity with an opportunity to get back on their feet by working in the production and sales of healthy, nourishing nut butters. Whether transitioning out of homelessness or work in the sex industry or battling mental illness, we work with each woman to help them earn an income, gain confidence, and achieve their goals. It's easy for people to confuse us for a nonprofit. But rather than spend time and energy on fundraising, we create quality products that, in turn, create dignified jobs while also providing an opportunity for mentorship and training.

At Ground Up, women gain experience in whichever areas of the business most interest them, from production and order fulfillment, to sales and marketing. Lately our production days have consisted of a team of ten women excelling in their various roles—from blending the nut butters in our huge standing mixer to navigating the complexities of our filling machine to toasting tray after tray of coconut, to labeling and dating each jar (which we still do by hand).

We meet each woman where they are at when they join the team and work with them to guide them toward their individual goals. For some, this may be as straightforward as learning to be reliable and show up to work on time. For others, that goal may be moving on to full-time employment with benefits. Our goal is to create a space that anyone can walk into no matter the challenges they have faced and help them feel a sense of new beginning and continuing encouragement.

We don't think there is a better feeling than looking around the kitchen and seeing our team of strong, motivated, and smart women *owning* their roles and working together to get the job done. We are endlessly inspired by the women behind Ground Up. The women who challenge us and push us to become better managers and business owners. The women who share their stories and their struggles and who do their best to shrug them off when they walk through the door for work. The women who have experienced hardship but are motivated each day to get up and make a positive change in their lives. You inspire us, and you keep us going. We dedicate this cookbook to you.

Our Food Philosophy

The recipes in this cookbook are a reflection of our personal diets. We feel best when eating whole, unprocessed foods. That's why we strive to make our nut butters without fillers or added oils. We are both lactose intolerant, so we avoid dairy; however, we are vegetable-loving omnivores. We avoid refined sugars, processed foods, and heavy carbohydrates in our diets, since we feel best when eating mostly proteins, fruits, vegetables, and healthy fats.

We've noticed increasing demand in the food world for healthier, plant-based recipes. From our friends and family to our customers, we talk to so many people who are seeking out healthy diets, such as Whole30 and the Paleo Diet, due to struggles with digestive issues, food intolerances, or just overall fatigue. We've found that folks love our products because they fit into their diet while providing them with an easy way to get their healthy fats and proteins—without sacrificing flavor!

In fact, before our products were available in stores, our friends on Whole30 would call us looking to get their fix from our sweetener-free almond and cashew butters. Friends would text us their orders, and we'd meet them in parking lots and outside our houses to "exchange the goods." Fortunately for everyone involved, our products are now in enough grocery stores that we don't have to personally deliver or meet up for seemingly shady exchanges.

We believe that everyone's body is unique, and what works for us may not work for you. (In fact, the two of us have different constitutions and find that the same meal will affect us each differently.) The most important thing is to listen to your body. We must treat our bodies with care and respect and tune in to the signals that they're sending us. We believe that food should be thoroughly enjoyed and appreciated and that it is important to take the time to truly taste and chew the food we're eating. (That being said, we'll be the first to admit that we sometimes eat a rushed lunch in our cars on busy days . . . we're not saying we're perfect!)

We both feel it's important to know where your food is coming from. Shopping at local farmers' markets, carefully reading labels, and making your own sauces and dressings at home are simple ways to be more in touch with the food that you're eating. We also look to support other local businesses like ourselves. While you may spend a few dollars more, it's worth it to have an impact on the local economy—and oftentimes to have a connection with who is making your food.

We try to use ingredients in our recipes that we keep on hand in our homes—focusing on ingredients that have not been overly processed, and avoiding any ingredients that are substitutes for other things. (For example, instead of using processed vegan butter, we'll opt for coconut oil or ghee.)

While some of the recipes in this book use harder-to-find ingredients, we try to keep each ingredient list as approachable as possible, with notes so that you can substitute or adjust based on what you have on hand. Chapter 9 contains reference information about selecting pantry ingredients. It's our hope that you can make each of these recipes your own. You are welcome to swap out any other nut butter for the one that we've listed in the recipe, and we encourage you to get creative with your flavor combos, using our recipes as a foundation and an inspiration.

Why Add Nut Butters to Your Diet?

Incorporating nut butters into your diet not only adds a healthy source of essential vitamins and minerals but also provides an easy way to add flavor and texture to dishes.

HEALTH

Let's talk about those *good* fats we know and love. While nut butters have a high fat content, they are composed of good fats—the monounsaturated and polyunsaturated fatty acids—that can actually help to lower your cholesterol and thus lower the risk of heart disease and type 2 diabetes. Feeling good about this nut butter journey you're embarking on? Yeah, you should!

In addition, nut butters are calorie-dense, making them an excellent way to get a quick energy burst in the midst of a ski adventure, a backpacking trip, or just a busy workday. Packed with protein, they also make a good post-workout snack for muscle recovery.

The nutrients in each nut (and nut butter) varies, but all nuts contain essential vitamins and minerals that aren't found in many other food sources. These include manganese, calcium, magnesium, fiber, and vitamin E.

It's also worth noting that nut butters can actually help you fight obesity and lose weight. Because of their ability to stabilize blood sugars, eating nut butters will provide you with more energy—and greater self-control over food cravings. They will also keep you feeling full for longer.

FLAVOR

Don't get us wrong, the health stuff is important—but the real reason we enjoy eating nut butters is their delicious and complex flavors. Trust us, adding a dollop of nut butter can provide all of the flavor you need in a dish, particularly if it's a nut butter that's already lightly sweetened and spiced. Simply adding a spoonful into oatmeal, smoothies, and even savory dishes can lend an appetizing flavor, quickly and easily. You can also treat nut butters like a condiment, drizzling them atop everything from fruit to avocado toast to roasted vegetables.

Since nuts contain natural sugars and are naturally sweet, enjoying nut butters is a wonderful way to quell your sweet tooth. Not only do they taste decadent and luxurious but enjoying a spoonful is oftentimes all you need to satiate any sweet cravings!

Due to their creaminess, nut butters make a great substitute in dairy-free and gluten-free cooking and baking. For instance, we love to swap out butter for nut butter in many baked goods recipes, as you'll see in our Apple Crisp (page 144) and our Almond Layer Cake with Cardamom Frosting + Cacao Nibs (page 159). They also add texture and variety to dishes. They can be used to thicken a simple dish like soup, such as in our Almond Butter Miso Soup (page 124) or Maple Walnut Spice Oatmeal (page 68).

SERVING SIZE

While we know it's easy to sit and eat an entire jar of nut butter in one sitting, by the spoonful (no judgment, we've done it before), it is not recommended. They are quite calorie-dense and should not be consumed in exceedingly large quantities.

When incorporating nut butters into your diet, note that the recommended serving size is 1 ounce, or around 2 tablespoons. While it varies by nut, this amount typically contains 160 to 200 calories, approximately 4 grams of protein, and approximately 16 grams of fat.

How to Use This Cookbook

We intend for this book to be a guide to those looking to make their own nut butter, as well as to incorporate more nut butter into their lives. We hope that you come away with the tools and know-how to make your own nut butters, as well as some helpful tips and recipes on how to use them in your everyday cooking.

Beginning with the basics of grinding nut butters, we'll share tips for buying, storing, and toasting your own nuts. We'll then move into various recipes for making your own nut butters at home. (The only tool you need is a food processor!) We'll then shift into how to enjoy nut butters, including fifty-plus sweet and savory recipes that incorporate them.

Next to each recipe, you'll find different icons to indicate dietary notes, as follows:

GLUTEN-FREE + DAIRY-FREE

VEGAN / VEGAN OPTION

SUGAR-FREE + WHOLE30

PALEO + KETOGENIC

All of the recipes in this book are dairy-free and peanut-free, and most are also sugar-free and gluten-free. Many also have a vegan option.

DAIRY-FREE

Neither of us can tolerate dairy, and since we recognize that we are not alone in this, we have kept all of the recipes in this cookbook dairy-free. Some of our recipes contain dairy substitutes, such as ghee (clarified butter) or almond milk, and you are more than welcome to replace those with their respective dairy products (butter and milk).

PEANUT-FREE

As a culture we tend to be very peanut-centric (we dare you to find a kid who doesn't know what a PB&J is!), so we are trying to mix it up and make it easier to expand beyond peanuts.

All of our recipes will be peanut- and peanut butter–free, since we recognize that there is a growing number of peanut allergies and many people look to tree nuts, such as almonds, cashews, walnuts, and hazelnuts as an alternative. In addition, diets such as Whole30 prohibit legumes, including peanuts.

Peanuts are not nuts. They are legumes and grow underground, meaning that they are exposed to fungus and mold that tree nuts are not. Peanuts have been found to contain high levels of aflatoxin, a carcinogen that is produced by a naturally occurring fungus in soil where peanuts are typically grown. Because almonds, cashews, and coconut are tree nuts and grown aboveground, they are not as susceptible to this toxic fungus.

We believe that it is healthy to eat a wide variety of different foods, and that diversity in diet is important for nutrient absorption.

REFINED SUGAR–FREE

Cane sugar is highly processed and contains no nutritional benefits. Most sugar crops are sprayed with pesticides, and then refined, meaning that it is chemically treated to remove color and impurities, thus stripping it of any nutrients. We use honey, maple syrup, coconut palm sugar, and dates as our primary sweeteners throughout this cookbook. And the only sweetener we add to a few of our Ground Up nut butters is honey!

GLUTEN-FREE

Most of our recipes are gluten-free, and grain-free where possible. While we are not gluten-intolerant ourselves, we recognize that many individuals are, and we find that our bodies feel better when we limit our gluten intake. That being said, some recipes include an option for gluten, such as our Almond Butter Udon Noodles (page 131) and Creamy Fennel "Alfredo" (page 134).

VEGAN

Despite the high number of plant-based recipes you'll find in this cookbook, we are not vegan or vegetarian. We personally find that small amounts of animal protein are good for our bodies from time to time and provide essential nutrients that are difficult to get elsewhere. You will find a few meat recipes in this book—including our Warm Hazelnut-Bacon Salad (page 119) and Marinated Chicken Skewers (page 121).

HONEY

You will also notice that we use honey as a sweetener in many recipes. While many of our vegan customers are fine with a bit of honey (especially if it is raw and local), we recognize that this isn't true for everyone. We therefore added an icon next to recipes that are nearly vegan, with the exception of honey, labeled "Vegan Option." In any recipe, including the nut butters, you can substitute maple syrup for honey to make it vegan.

In all that we do, we aim to show you that truly healthy food can also taste like a decadent treat, and in all of our recipes, we aim to surprise and delight your taste buds. We constantly have customers and friends telling us, "This tastes so good; I just want to eat it by the spoonful—surely it can't be healthy?!" We hope that the recipes in this cookbook leave you feeling the same way.

You won't find a classic PB&J recipe in this cookbook. Instead, we use nut butters as the building blocks for complex flavors, from sauces to baked goods. Get ready to think about nut butter like you never have before.

CHAPTER TWO:

Guide to Nuts + Nut Butters

We have made *countless* nut butters over the years. While we've had some major hits (Cinnamon Snickerdoodle was a happy accident), there have also been some, well . . . stranger concoctions (don't ever make balsamic or lime nut butter). We love tinkering in our kitchen with a variety of different nuts and flavors, and we want to show you how to unleash your creativity to create nut butters. We'll share some basic recipes, as well as some more complex flavors, but first let's talk about nuts.

The Building Blocks: Nuts + Seeds

Nuts are an excellent source of healthy fats, including omega-6s. They are also high in protein, making them an excellent source for vegetarians and vegans. Nuts are loaded with vitamins and minerals, including calcium and magnesium.

Information on the best nuts and seeds to transform into nut butters follows:

ALMONDS

Almonds are one of the most versatile and nutritious nuts. They are grown commercially in the United States (and rank as the seventh-largest U.S. food export). While historically grown in the Mediterranean region, California is now the world's largest producer of almonds, accounting for 80 percent of the world's supply. What we consider to be an almond "nut" is in technicality *not* a nut—rather, it is the seed of an almond tree.

Almonds are an excellent source of vitamin E, magnesium, riboflavin, and manganese. In comparison with peanut butter, a single serving of almond butter contains three times as much vitamin E, twice as much iron, and seven times more calcium. It also contains twice as much fiber, with roughly 3.3 grams in 2 tablespoons, compared with just 1.6 grams in peanut butter.

Almonds are delicately flavored, slightly sweet, and buttery. They are great paired with both sweet and savory flavors, making them a wonderful base nut. We love plain Almond Butter (page 44) as a substitute for peanut butter or as a base in sauces, soups, and dressings.

Nutty Nugget: Romans once considered almonds to be a fertility charm and presented them to newlyweds as a gift.

BRAZIL NUTS

Despite their name, Brazil nuts are produced primarily in Bolivia. These large tree nuts have a smooth and shiny exterior and a high fat content. Their texture is creamy, and they taste rich and sweet—and a bit like coconut.

Brazil nuts are the number one food source for selenium, an important nutrient for everything from skin health to thyroid function to fighting inflammation.

Brazil nut butter is creamy and delicious, perfect for both sweet and savory uses.

Nutty Nugget: Brazil nut trees can grow up to 200 feet tall, and a single tree can produce as much as 250 pounds in a year. It's illegal to cut down a Brazil nut tree in Brazil because they are becoming endangered.

CASHEWS

The creamiest of all the tree nuts, cashews are rich in vitamins and minerals. Native to Brazil, the majority of these kidney-shaped nuts are now grown in India, the Ivory Coast, and Vietnam.

Despite their creamy texture, cashews actually have a lower fat content (but higher protein content) in comparison with other nuts. They are a rich source of copper, phosphorus, magnesium, and manganese—with a single serving containing greater than 75 percent of the recommended daily value of each. Cashews also contain biotin, which is great for hair, skin, and nails.

In flavor, cashew nuts are sweet, creamy, and rich—making them an excellent complement to more bitter nuts, such as hazelnuts and walnuts.

Nutty Nugget: Cashew nuts come from a pear-shaped fruit called the cashew apple. The nut grows outside of the

fruit, hanging down below it. While you'd be hard-pressed to find a cashew apple in the U.S., they grow abundantly in Brazil, where they are considered a delicacy.

COCONUT

Coconut is primarily grown and produced in Indonesia, the Philippines, and India—and if you ever have a chance to visit one of these countries to enjoy juice from a freshly cracked-open coconut, do it.

High in fiber and saturated fats, coconut also has a considerable amount of manganese, which is an essential nutrient for brain and nervous system functioning.

We add coconut to a few of our nut butters—not only for its rich flavor but also for the texture it provides. We find that coconut helps to maintain a smoother, more liquid consistency—especially if we are adding in a dry spice or powder, such as cinnamon or cocoa powder. Adding coconut, which naturally releases a more liquidy oil when ground up, helps the nut butter maintain a spreadable texture.

Since coconut butter is high in saturated fat, it will harden at room temperature. If you've made a nut butter with coconut in it and notice that it is quite solid, simply warm it in the microwave or on the stovetop to bring it to a spreadable consistency. We don't recommend storing coconut-based nut butters in the refrigerator. In the winter months, try to store them in a warmer location, such as above a stovetop or near a furnace. The benefit of coconut's high saturated fat content is that it is highly stable and won't go rancid as easily as some of the other nuts.

Shopping Tip: When buying coconut, always look for unsweetened—and when you're buying it to make nut butter, we recommend shredded over the larger coconut flakes.

Nutty Nugget: The coconut got its name from sixteenth-century Spanish and Portuguese explorers who thought its appearance resembled the face of the "coco," a folkloric monster.

HAZELNUTS

Did you know that 99 percent of hazelnuts grown in the United States are grown in Oregon? Remarkably, this is only

5 percent of the world's crop, with Turkey as the largest producer by far.

Hazelnuts are an excellent source of vitamin E and manganese, as well as rich in folate, fiber, and copper.

They are very distinct in flavor, slightly bitter, and yet warming. For this reason, we recommend pairing hazelnuts with sweeter flavors, such as honey, chocolate, and cashew (check out our Chocolate-Hazelnut Cashew Butter [page 58]), or playing up their bitterness in more savory dishes—for instance, in our Warm Hazelnut-Bacon Salad (page 119).

Nutty Nugget: There is debate as to the true name of the hazelnut—we are often told it is actually called a "filbert," as it is more commonly known in Europe. The origin of that name? Celebration day for France's St. Philbert is August 20, the same time of year when hazelnuts are ready to be harvested and thus widely enjoyed.

MACADAMIA NUTS

Oh, how we wish we lived in a climate where macadamia nuts were native! These deliciously buttery, smooth, and crunchy nuts are grown in tropical climates, such as South Africa, Australia, and Hawaii.

Macadamia nuts are high in monounsaturated fats, fiber, and thiamin. They have the highest fat content of all the tree nuts, at 80 percent. They are also rich in magnesium, copper, iron, and zinc.

Macadamia nuts are rich and buttery with hints of tropical flavor reminiscent to coconut or cashews.

Nutty Nugget: Macadamia nuts are the most expensive nut in the world, since only a limited number of fruits are produced by a single tree per season, and the outer shell is very hard to crack.

PECANS

Pecans are the only major tree nut that is native to North America, with 80 percent grown in the U.S., primarily in Georgia. Considered the pride of the South, these buttery-rich nuts contain 70 percent fat and are rich in fiber.

Pecans are a rich source of magnesium, phosphorus, zinc, thiamin, and particularly high in manganese. They are also high in calcium, iron, selenium, and B vitamins.

Delicate and buttery, pecans are similar to walnuts but much sweeter. Due to their high fat content, these will go rancid sooner than other nuts, so we recommend storing in a glass jar in the refrigerator.

Nutty Nugget: The word "pecan" comes from an Algonquin word meaning "nut requiring a stone to crack."

PISTACHIOS

While the U.S. is the world's largest producer of pistachios (most of which are grown in California), Iran is a close second.

If you've ever had the pleasure of enjoying a freshly toasted and perfectly salted pistachio, you may be surprised to learn that they are actually healthy for you, as well. Pistachios are high in fiber, as well as a good source of vitamin B6, which many don't get enough of in their diet. They are rich in potassium, with 1 ounce containing more potassium than half of a banana.

Pistachios taste mildly sweet and savory, but their most distinctive feature is their bright-green color.

Nutty Nugget: In India, pistachios are prized for their warming qualities; they believe pistachios can heat the body when eaten in large quantities during colder months.

PUMPKIN SEEDS

Native to North America, China is now the largest producer of pumpkin seeds (and pumpkins). They are rich in antioxidants, iron, zinc, magnesium, and omega-3s. Pumpkin seeds have a nutty, sweet flavor and a slightly chewy texture.

We find plain pumpkin seed butter to be thick in texture and a bit astringent in taste, so we prefer to mix ours with almonds and other nuts, such as in our Pumpkin Seed–Almond Butter (page 52).

Nutty Nugget: Pumpkin seeds are also called "pepitas"—a Mexican-Spanish term that comes from "pepita de calabaza," which means "little seed of squash."

SESAME SEEDS

The world's largest producers of sesame seeds are Tanzania, Myanmar, India, Sudan, and China. Sesame seeds are rich in calcium, iron, magnesium, potassium, and fiber.

This feels like a big statement to make, but we are perhaps as obsessed with the sesame seed paste tahini as we are with nut butters. We love the mild, nutty, toasted flavor and incorporate it into dressings, sauces, and homemade hummus.

Nutty Nugget: Since tahini is the product of grinding up toasted sesame seeds until they form a paste, making tahini is essentially the same process as making nut butter. Which means that you can easily make tahini at home by following our instructions for making nut butter!

SUNFLOWER SEEDS

Sunflower seeds are primarily grown and produced in Russia and Ukraine. They are a rich source of vitamin E, thiamin, calcium, iron, magnesium, manganese, phosphorus, iron, and zinc.

Like pumpkin seeds, sunflowers seeds are a lower-cost alternative to many tree nuts. Adding a cup of sunflower seeds to nut butter is a healthy, delicious and cost-effective way to get more out of your nut butters.

Nutty Nugget: Sunflower seeds can help to regulate blood pressure since they contain all three nutrients most integral to regulation: calcium, potassium, and magnesium.

WALNUTS

Thirty-eight percent of the world's walnuts are grown in the U.S., primarily in California. The majority are grown in China, while Iran and Turkey are also large producers.

Walnuts are high in antioxidants and are particularly known for their high amount of heart-healthy omega-3s. Composed of 65 percent fat, they are lower in protein and carbohydrates than other nuts. As a result of their high fat content, they are more susceptible to rancidity than other nuts, so we recommend storing them in the refrigerator.

Walnuts are savory, rich, and buttery, but walnut butter on its own can taste quite bitter. We love their distinct taste balanced out with cashews in our Walnut-Cashew Butter (page 49).

Nutty Nugget: Walnuts were used by artists such as Leonardo da Vinci to make ink and oils for drawing and painting. Their pigments were also used to create fabric and hair dye.

Nut Butter: The Basics

We may be biased, but we think the process of making nut butter at home is one of the most fun and creative things to do in the kitchen. For one thing, when you toast nuts in the oven, your kitchen gets all toasty and fragrant, so you're already starting out with a win. It's fun to play around with different flavor combinations and taste them along the way. Really the best reason of all is that WARM NUT BUTTER IS THE BEST THING EVER. For real. Your food processor will make the butter so warm. It's so dangerously good we just want to lick it off the food processor. (But don't worry, we are more civilized than that . . . most of the time.)

Now that we've convinced you why you should make nut butter at home, let's buy the nuts, toast them, and make nut butters. The information in the following pages is based on our own personal research and preferences.

BUYING NUTS

Choose Raw

While you can find pre-toasted nuts in stores, we encourage you to buy raw nuts and do the toasting yourself. This not only ensures a fresher, nuttier taste but also avoids the added oils and refined salt that many pre-toasted nuts are prepared with.

Even though the packaging may say "raw," most commercially available nuts have been treated in some way, whether through pasteurization or blanching. Almonds, for instance, are required by law to be pasteurized to reduce the potential for pathogen contamination. This treatment shouldn't affect the health benefit of the nuts, but we do believe it's worth mentioning.

Blanching nuts is the process of removing the skins or husks from the outsides of nuts that are grown in a shell (for instance, almonds, hazelnuts, and walnuts). Buying blanched nuts means you won't have to remove any skins.

So when you're buying nuts, the main things you want to look for are *raw, shelled, blanched*, and *unsalted*.

Buy in Bulk

We find that buying nuts in bulk bins tends to be the most affordable option; however, you will want to be sure to try one first to ensure it has not gone bad. (Learn more about how to tell if a nut has gone bad in the next section.) Without a sealed package or expiration date, you'll want to be careful before purchasing. We recommend buying them from a trusted store that has a higher turnover of their bulk bin selection. (Truly, there is nothing sadder than splurging on nuts only to get home and realize that they are rancid. Learn from our mistakes!)

If you're looking for nuts that provide the best bang for your buck, try walnuts or almonds. In addition, pumpkin seeds or sunflower seeds are another cost-effective option.

Organic vs. Nonorganic

We often get asked whether our nuts are organic or not, and the topic is certainly a controversial one. We have found inconsistent data that organic nuts are actually lower in pesticides, though many believe that to be the case. Because nuts are shelled, some experts also say they are inherently more protected from the dangers of pesticides.

In addition, buying organic nuts can be difficult and expensive, in large part because there are so few organic nut farms. The process for farmers to get certified is long and cumbersome, and many do not have the resources to do so.

We opt for a mix of organic and nonorganic nuts in our blends, and value local farmer relationships more than an organic label. But ultimately, you must decide whether buying organic makes sense for your budget and values.

STORING NUTS

Due to their high fat content, nuts should be stored in a cool, dark, and dry place, and always in glass jars. The high oil content in nuts causes them to go rancid over time. Exposure to air, light, and heat, a process known as oxidation, will expedite this process, so proper storage is key.

Most nuts will keep for at least 3 months at room temperature, but, if you have the space, we recommend storing them in airtight glass jars in the refrigerator. They will keep for up to 6 months refrigerated or for up to 1 year in the freezer.

Nuts with a higher fat content—including pecans and walnuts—run the greatest risk of going rancid.

If you're unsure whether your nuts have gone rancid, first check to see if their odor and appearance is off. They may appear darker in color, or to have shriveled up a bit. However, the surest way to tell is through taste. Rancid nuts have a slightly sour, pungent flavor, and while they are not dangerous to eat, the taste is not pleasant.

Storage suggestions are the same for both raw and toasted nuts. If you've toasted your nuts and notice that they have lost their crispness while in storage, simply pop them back in the oven at 325°F for 5 minutes to revive them.

SOAKING NUTS (AND PHYTIC ACID)

Nuts contain phytic acid; designed to protect the seeds until germination, it cannot be easily digested by humans. But there are two ways to break down the phytic acid: soaking and toasting.

If we had all of the time in the world, perhaps we would soak and dehydrate our nuts. This method makes the nuts easier to digest, and makes their nutrients more readily available. However, this method is way more work than it sounds.

If you would like to soak your nuts, place them in a bowl of salt water overnight, or for at least 7 hours. Drain and then bake in a warm 150°F oven for 12 to 24 hours until crisp. (Although cashews shouldn't be soaked longer than 6 hours.)

Given the effort involved, we opt to toast our nuts instead, which also has the effect of increasing their digestibility and removing phytic acid. You'll find instructions for how to toast your own nuts in the next section.

RAW VS. TOASTED

Ah, yes, the raw versus toasted debate. We'll keep it short for you. We prefer the taste and depth of nut butters made with toasted nuts, but all of our recipes can be made with raw nuts, as well. The words "toasted" and "roasted" are often used interchangeably on food packaging and recipe instructions. For the sake of clarity, we stick with the term "toasting" in this book.

A Guide to Toasting Nuts

Toasting nuts not only increases their digestibility but also lends them a nice crunch, deepens their flavors, and makes them taste richer and more complex. Lastly, the process of toasting them releases their essential oils, creating a deliciously nutty aroma.

There are two commercial methods for toasting nuts—oil roasted or dry roasted (without oil). When making nut butter, we recommend dry roasting.

Always use **raw, shelled, unsalted nuts**. (If there is some skin on them, such as in the case of hazelnuts, that is perfectly fine.)

Make sure the **oven is preheated** before you add your pans.

Nuts should be toasted at **350°F** or according to the temperature guidelines in each recipe.

Always set a timer! It is *so easy* to burn nuts when you are toasting them. (Truly, we can't even count the number of times we've wasted a tray of nuts because we got distracted.)

Spread in a single, even layer. Never overcrowd the baking sheet.

Use a baking sheet. You don't want to trap in the moisture by using a pan with higher sides; you want them to get crispy. (No need to grease the pan or line it with paper, either—toasting nuts won't dirty your pan much at all!)

We also recommend toasting **one pan at a time**; it is not only easier to keep track of but also ensures even toasting for all nuts.

Use your nose. Scent is the biggest indicator of doneness, so pay attention. By the time you've smelled a pungent toasted smell, you've probably burnt your nuts.

Make sure to **toast the nuts in advance** of making the nut butter; you want the nuts to cool entirely before processing them into butter.

Underbake your nuts. Keep in mind that they will continue to cook for a bit longer when you remove them from the oven. (Plus, if you need to, you can throw them back in for a couple of minutes to crisp them up.)

If you notice that they are toasting unevenly, simply **give the nuts a stir halfway through.**

Chop nuts after you've toasted and cooled them.

Remove skins after toasting. Hazelnuts, pistachios, and Brazil nuts have skins on them, and you will want to do your best to remove these after toasting. Our preferred method is to place them in a clean, dry kitchen towel and rub vigorously; the skins should come right off if they have been toasted long enough.

NUT / SEED	TOASTING TEMP	TOASTING AMOUNT	TOASTING TIME	SIGNS OF DONENESS
Almonds (Whole)	350°F	4 cups	10 to 12 min	• Fragrant smell • Crackling noise • Slightly darker shell • Golden brown in the center
Brazil Nuts	350°F	3 cups	10 to 12 min	• Fragrant smell • Skins will start to peel off easily
Cashews (Halves + Pieces)	350°F	4 cups	5 to 7 min	• Fragrant smell • Golden brown color
Coconut (Medium Shredded Unsweetened)	350°F	3 cups	2 to 3 min	• Fragrant smell • Golden brown
Hazelnuts (Whole + Pieces)	350°F	4 cups	10 to 12 min	• Fragrant smell • Golden brown in the center • Skins will start to peel off easily
Macadamia Nuts	350°F	4 cups	12 to 15 min	• Fragrant smell • Golden brown in color
Pecans (Halves + Pieces)	350°F	4 cups	5 to 7 min	• Fragrant smell • Crackling sound
Pistachios (Shelled)	350°F	4 cups	6 to 8 min	• Fragrant smell • Skins will start to peel off easily
Pumpkin Seeds	350°F	3 cups	3 to 4 min	• Crackling sound • Slightly brown
Sesame Seeds	350°F	3 cups	4 to 5 min	• Fragrant smell • Slightly darker color
Sunflower Seeds	350°F	3 cups	2 to 3 min	• Crackling sound • Slightly darker color
Walnuts (Halves + Pieces)	350°F	4 cups	6 to 8 min	• Fragrant smell • Slightly darker color • Crackling noise

Please Note + IF YOU ARE TOASTING LESS THAN THE AMOUNT LISTED ABOVE, YOUR TOASTING TIME MAY BE SHORTER.

How to Make Nut Butters

So at this point, you've learned how to toast nuts, you're inspired by hearing how fun and creative it is to make nut butters, and you're convinced that you need more nut butter in your life. Are we right?!

Let's get down to it, then. We are going to share all of the tips and tricks to help you make your own nut butters at home, from the equipment you'll need to some unique and delicious flavor combos.

TOOLS + EQUIPMENT

There is only one tool that you will need for making nut butters, and that is a decent food processor. Your food processor should have a bowl capacity of at least 7 cups. (We use a 16-cup processor, which is the maximum available before you get into industrial equipment.)

We wanted to address a couple questions that we often get asked:

Q. *I don't own a food processor, and they seem expensive. Any suggestions?*

A. If you don't already own a food processor and aren't ready to splurge on one, we encourage you to ask around in your community. We were surprised by how many of our friends and family had older-model food processors sitting around that they never actually used . . . in most cases a wedding gift that was still taking up space that they were happy to let us borrow. And the food processor doesn't need to be the most high-tech; it just needs to be large enough, and still have a sharp enough blade to get the job done. In addition, you could try Goodwill, or your local resale shop, for used machines; we've spotted some great deals.

A standard blender won't cut it, but we have heard that you can make them in a Vitamix. We expect that the texture will be a bit different than in a food processor but encourage you to give it a go if you already have a Vitamix. Please note that if you're going to try this method, the timing and instructions that we've provided for grinding may need to be adjusted.

Q. *Can I use a food chopper or a mini-prep food processor?*

A. Unfortunately, it is unlikely that these will work for nut butters. You need the motor to have significant power (ideally at least 400 watts).

The food processor is an invaluable tool for us, and you will see that we use it not only for making nut butters but also for preparing sauces (such as Creamy Vegan "Alfredo" Sauce, on page 108), dips (such as Muhammara [Walnut Red Pepper Dip], on page 114), and snacks (such as Bliss Balls, Three Ways, on page 93).

Back in the early days of our business, we produced all of our nut butters in countertop food processors. In fact, Julie's parents were the first—and, to date, the only people—to "invest" in our business, by purchasing a brand-new, full-size, state-of-the-art food processor for us. We would line up our food processors in a row on "production days"—which were really just evenings spent at one of our homes after our day jobs—jarring as much nut butter as we could until we couldn't keep our eyes open any longer.

This is when we learned that home food processors have their limits, and we really pushed ours. It can take up to 15 minutes for the nuts to grind into a butter. During that time, the machines may get quite warm. If you are making several nut butters in a row, your food processor runs the risk of overheating and powering off momentarily.

To avoid a shutdown:

1. Give your machine a rest in between batches.
2. Don't exceed the capacity. In most cases, the maximum capacity for dried foods or nuts is less than the total bowl capacity. For instance, we have a 16-cup food processor, but the machine's maximum capacity for nuts is only 6 cups. (We have tried to push the limits on these maximums, and, trust us, they're stated for a reason. We have burnt out many machines.)
3. If necessary, use ice packs! Really, though, you shouldn't need to do this. But, back in the day, if our machines were getting too hot and we had a large production run, we would strap ice packs around them to cool them down.

HOW-TO GUIDE

In each of the ten nut butter recipes you'll find in the next chapter, there will be step-by-step instructions; however, if you've never made nut butter before, we recommend reading through the following steps to familiarize yourself with the process.

Step 1: Choose Your Base Nut(s)

Feel free to choose a single nut variety or opt for a blend of various nuts. Either way, we recommend you use at least 3 and no more than 6 cups of nuts. (You need at least 3 cups in the food processor to ensure that there is enough for the blade to stick to.) If you're looking for base flavor inspiration, see pages 40 and 41.

We recommend toasting your nuts beforehand (see page 29), but make sure the nuts have cooled down before you add them to the food processor bowl.

Step 2: Grind into a Nut Butter

Add the nuts and sea salt to the food processor. (As a starting point, assume ¼ teaspoon of salt per 1 cup of nuts. It's also fine not to salt your nut butter, but we find it really enhances the flavor.)

Turn your food processor on to process the nuts and sea salt. You'll want to make sure to process them for as long as it takes for the natural oils in the nuts to release, forming a beautiful butter. It may seem like it will never get there, but have faith. The speed of each food processor can vary, so the processing times will, as well. The speed also varies by nut.

Here's a more detailed overview of what to expect:

First, you'll hear a loud (and somewhat obnoxious) noise as the food processor initially chops up the nuts into smaller pieces. (Don't worry, this loud phase won't last long.)

Second, you'll hear the nuts start to crumble into finer pieces, essentially a nut flour. Listen to the whirring of the food processor blade as it continues to break the nuts down.

In some cases, you'll notice a large ball of "dough" forming inside the food processor. This is normal; simply continue to let it process.

If you notice that the nuts keep getting stuck on the side of the processor, and they are not moving down into the blade area, open the top of the machine and use a spatula to scrape down the insides of the machine. You may need to scrape a few times during the process, or sometimes not at all.

Continue to process for as long as it takes for the nuts to turn into nut butter. This time can range from 4 to 20 minutes.

You will know that your nut butter is done by the sound and the texture.

Texturally, the nuts should have released into a beautiful liquid butter. (For seed butters, the texture is more like a thick paste than a liquid.)

You should actually *hear* that the nut butter is done from the sudden quiet that takes over the kitchen. It's almost as if the nuts "give in" and release, and so the blade doesn't have any resistance against it anymore, and you can just hear its quiet hum.

If you let it run for a long enough time, you may hear a splashing sound—and you'll see the liquid nut butter splashing against the sides of the machine. (This is more often the case with coconut-based nut butters, because coconut is naturally quite oily.) This means your nut butter is most certainly done, and it should be extremely smooth and creamy!

Step 3: Add In Your Flavorings

This is where you get to transform your basic nut butter into a culinary masterpiece—and create the nut butter of your dreams.

Of course, sometimes you just want a basic nut butter for everyday use (like Almond Butter, on page 44). If you prefer keeping yours simple, no need to add flavors or sweeteners. Skip right on to Step 6—if you want some crunch—or simply jar it up as is.

If you're interested in taking your nut butters to the next level, we recommend adding one (or five) of the following:

Spices + Adding spice to nut butter is one of our favorite things. Always use ground spices (freshly ground in your own spice grinder is the most flavorful method). Even though you are putting the spice in a food processor, it won't be able to chop up, say, a cardamom pod or cinnamon stick. You'll need something with a finer grind. Here are our favorite spices to add, in order from sweet to savory:

+ CINNAMON
+ CARDAMOM
+ CLOVE
+ NUTMEG
+ ALLSPICE
+ ANISE
+ GINGER
+ TURMERIC
+ CHILI POWDER
+ CAYENNE
+ CUMIN
+ CORIANDER
+ BLACK PEPPER
+ FENUGREEK

Vanilla Bean + Vanilla is known to naturally enhance other flavors, and in this case, it brings out the sweetness of the nuts in a beautiful way. Adding just ½ teaspoon of vanilla extract (or seeds from half of a vanilla bean) will do wonders for your nut butter flavor.

Oils + Extracts + Any essential oil or extract can be added to nut butter, from almond extract to rosewater. Get creative with this—but note that too much liquid could change the texture of your nut butter, so we recommend no more than 1 teaspoon per 3-cup batch of nut butter. (And if using essential oils, just a few small drops will do the trick.) Some suggestions for oils and extracts that we like to use include:

+ PURE VANILLA EXTRACT (DISCUSSED ABOVE)
+ PURE ALMOND EXTRACT
+ PEPPERMINT EXTRACT OR 100 PERCENT PURE PEPPERMINT OIL
+ 100 PERCENT PURE BERGAMOT OIL *(IT TASTES JUST LIKE EARL GREY!)*
+ ROSEWATER

Tip: When selecting oils, always make sure that they are in fact composed of only a single ingredient (you are looking for 100 percent pure food-safe oil).

Dried Flowers + Herbs + Teas + Adding dried flowers, herbs, and teas is a unique way to flavor your nut butters, while adding a lovely fragrance to them, as well. We don't recommend using fresh flowers or herbs due to their high water content. The nut butter will not keep as long. Dried is a must! The one thing worth noting here, though, is that you may find it hard to gauge how much to add to a batch, as the flavor will change and seep in more over time. We recommend starting with 1 to 2 tablespoons and then tasting as you go. Keep in mind that it may intensify over time. Some examples of flowers, herbs, and teas we like to add are:

+ LAVENDER BUDS *(WE USE THESE IN OUR LAVENDER HONEY NUT BUTTER)*
+ ROSE PETALS
+ ROSEMARY
+ MINT
+ BLACK TEA *(ONE OF OUR FAVORITE SEASONAL FLAVORS WAS AN EARL GREY FLAVOR WE DID WITH SMITH TEA!)*
+ CHAI TEA BLENDS
+ ROOIBOS (RED TEA)
+ DRIED ORANGE PEEL

Powders † Powdered foods and mixes are an easy way to add flavor to nut butter. Add a tablespoon to your batch and you'll likely get all of the flavor you need. Below are some ideas for different powders you could add, though keep in mind that powders tend to absorb a lot of the moisture, creating a thicker nut butter. You may also want to add a tablespoon of coconut oil to thin it out.

+ MATCHA GREEN TEA POWDER
+ INSTANT ESPRESSO POWDER
+ UNSWEETENED 100 PERCENT COCOA POWDER

Chocolate † While we try to keep our nut butters sweetener-free, you could also add chocolate or chocolate chips. Processing the chocolate in with the warm nut butter for a few minutes should melt it, giving you a smooth, rich, and chocolaty nut butter. We prefer to add cocoa powder or cacao nibs and a natural sweetener to ours; if you're feeling decadent, going this route is never a bad idea!

Learn from Our Mistakes: We also wanted to mention what doesn't work for flavors, based on our experience. As mentioned, don't add any liquids more than a small amount of oil or extract. We tried adding balsamic vinegar—and initially the results were *amazing*! So tasty on the first day. But when we went to try it on the second day, it was completely inedible and sour. We also recommend avoiding fresh citrus zests and juice, fresh ginger, or any fresh fruit. (We once made a sesame and lime zest nut butter that also turned out to be terrible.) If you do add any of these ingredients, note that the shelf life will be considerably shorter and you will want to keep it refrigerated.

Step 4: Add In Your Sweeteners

Sweeteners are also completely optional; however, they are another way to add flavor to your nut butters—and round out the flavor profile for a more enjoyable spoonful. We prefer not to add in any refined sugars (e.g., cane sugar, powdered sugar, agave, and corn syrup), instead opting to sweeten our nut butters with a small amount of honey or another natural sweetener. Try adding in flavored honeys, such as smoked honey, for an added flavor boost.

Below is a list of the sweeteners we recommend trying. Start with a tablespoon, and add more from there!

+ RAW HONEY—*THIS IS OUR GO-TO!*
+ PURE MAPLE SYRUP
+ PITTED, DRIED DATES, OR DATE SYRUP
+ COCONUT SUGAR

Step 5: Process Again until Smooth

After adding in your sweetener and flavorings, it's time to start grinding again. The second grind allows the flavors to incorporate, and you may notice that the texture will change. In some cases, it will come together quickly into nut butter again (for instance, if you are only adding a bit of spice, it could take 30 seconds to incorporate), but in others, it will take longer. The second grind could take up to 10 minutes, depending on what you have added in. You may notice that the beautiful nut butter you just created has broken down and is now clumped into a ball again; that is fine—we promise it will turn back into nut butter. If it seems to be struggling to come together and is just a troublesome blob, we suggest adding a tablespoon of coconut oil as a means of helping it to smooth out.

At this point, we suggest tasting and adjusting as needed. Perhaps it needs more salt, more honey, or a bit more spice. You get to decide!

Step 6: Add Textural Mix-Ins

The final step here is also optional, and really, it comes down to a decision of whether you would like your nut butter to be chunky or smooth. (We have learned that people have firm opinions on this matter.)

If you would like your nut butter to be smooth, then you are done. Move on to Step 7. If you would like your nut butter to be chunky in texture, read on.

Once your nut butter is finished, you can quickly pulse in textural crunch. Here are some suggestions:

Toasted Nuts + Seeds + This makes for a classically "crunchy" nut butter. Pulse the nuts until they are broken up into small pieces but haven't dissolved into nut butter, around 15 to 30 seconds. For instance, if you want chunky almond butter, set aside a half cup of toasted almonds to add in at the very end.

Dried Fruit + Incorporate raisins, cranberries, currants, goji berries, and other dried fruits by quickly pulsing in around a half cup until they are dispersed throughout the nut butter. This should take between 5 to 15 seconds.

Other Mix-Ins + Granola, cacao nibs, chia seeds, and crystallized ginger are some of our favorite finishes.

Sea Salt + For our "salted" nut butters, we go light on our base salt and quickly pulse in a sea salt at the end. This ensures delicate salt crystals in every spoonful (and satisfies our salt-addicted palates). We use flaky sea salt for finishing dishes.

Step 7: Jar 'Em Up

Transfer your nut butter to a clean, dry glass jar, and keep the delicious drizzles left in the food processor and on the blade for yourself. At this point, you've earned it.

Keep glass mason jars on hand for storing your nut butters. And check out our tips on storing nut butter on the following page.

FLAVOR INSPIRATION

We trust that you are wildly creative and already have ideas ping-ponging around in your mind for what deliciousness you will create. For those days when you need a little extra creativity, here's a list of a few places to start:

Smoked Honey, Cinnamon, and Raisin: Use a standard almond base, add in a scoop of smoked honey and a dash of cinnamon, and pulse in raisins at the end.

Matcha Rose: Use a coconut butter base, adding in matcha powder and dried rose petals.

Chocolate-Granola: Use a cashew butter base, then add in cocoa powder and coconut sugar, swirling in cacao nibs and granola at the end.

Rosemary Almond: Use an almond base and take it in a savory direction, adding in olive oil, dried rosemary, or pure rosemary oil, and a dash of garlic powder.

Gingerbread: Use a hazelnut and almond base, then add in molasses, ground ginger, cinnamon, and chunks of candied ginger at the end.

Chai Spice: We actually put a recipe for this at the end of our Cardamom Almond-Cashew Butter recipe (page 47).

Birthday Cake: This is a fun one to gift to friends on their birthdays or to make in celebration. Use a cashew butter base and add coconut sugar and *imitation* vanilla extract, then swirl in confetti sprinkles. (The "imitation" is key because it lends the classic Funfetti flavor.)

Fenugreek Walnut: Another, more savory option; start with a walnut-cashew base, then blend in ground fenugreek and maple syrup.

STORING NUT BUTTERS

While many brands advise storing your nut butter in the refrigerator, nut butters are actually a shelf-stable product. Nut butters containing coconut (such as our Cinnamon Snickerdoodle) will harden when refrigerated. With other nut butters, however, you are welcome to store them in the refrigerator if that suits you.

Separation is natural. If you notice that the oils have risen to the top of the jar, simply stir. (Especially if you have coconut in it and the top is white, it's normal.) In cooler months, if you notice that your nut butter is quite hard, you can zap it in the microwave for 15 to 20 seconds to make it more liquefied. Not a fan of the microwave? You can also warm up your nut butter by heating it slightly on the stovetop, placing your jar in a bowl of warm water before stirring.

We know we've mentioned it before, but it's important: Water is the enemy of nut butter and is the surest way to make your nut butter mold or go rancid.

CHAPTER THREE:

Nut Butter Recipes

Narrowing down our top ten nut butter recipes was no easy feat. Our goal with these recipes is to provide a foundation for different types and to inspire you to get creative in making your own. We're sharing some of our top-secret Ground Up recipes, as well as some others that we enjoy at home (We think you will, too!).

Almond Butter

Makes 2 cups (16 ounces)

If you're a plain Jane, creamy Jif kinda gal, this is the nut butter for you. It's also a great base recipe for baking and cooking with, and it's the perfect substitute for your classic peanut butter.

And since we're not personally the best at keeping it simple (we always fight the temptation to add a little something extra for pizzazz), we encourage you to get creative with this one! If you'd like it to be chunky, simply pulse in toasted nuts at the very end. If you'd like it to be sweet, add a tablespoon of honey or maple syrup. Or add your favorite spice—cinnamon or nutmeg pair deliciously with almonds.

3 CUPS UNSALTED ALMONDS, TOASTED

1 TEASPOON SEA SALT

1. Place the almonds and sea salt in a food processor fitted with a metal S-shaped blade.
2. Process until the consistency is completely smooth, approximately 5 to 15 minutes depending on the power of the food processor's motor. If the nuts get stuck to the sides, pause the machine and use a rubber spatula to scrape them down as many times as needed. The nut butter is done when the texture is smooth and runny, the blade glides easily through the mixture, and there are no longer any chunks.
3. Transfer the mixture to two (8-ounce) glass jars. The nut butter will keep for 1 year without refrigeration. If the oils naturally separate over time, simply stir to incorporate.

Note + **THIS IS A BASE RECIPE THAT YOU COULD USE FOR ANY TYPE OF NUT BUTTER, FROM BRAZIL NUT TO CASHEW. PLEASE NOTE THAT THE PROCESSING SPEED MAY VARY DEPENDING ON THE NUT.**

GLUTEN-FREE + DAIRY-FREE + VEGAN + REFINED SUGAR–FREE + WHOLE30 + PALEO + KETO

GROUND
UP

Cardamom Almond–Cashew Butter

Makes 2 cups (16 ounces)

We still remember making this nut butter for the first time in our home food processor—the smell of cardamom warming the kitchen; the warm spice blending so beautifully with the rich and creamy nut butter. It's the recipe that made us realize how decadent nut butter could be.

The almond-cashew base provides a natural sweetness and creaminess that pairs nicely with the strong, complex cardamom flavor. If you aren't familiar with cardamom, it is an incredibly versatile spice that you'll find starring in everything from Turkish coffee to Scandinavian baked goods to Indian curry dishes.

Perhaps its versatility is why our cardamom flavor continues to be our favorite—we love it swirled into our morning oatmeal, blended into a savory noodle sauce, or simply paired with a piece of fruit!

2½ CUPS UNSALTED ALMONDS, TOASTED

1½ CUPS UNSALTED CASHEWS, TOASTED

1½ TEASPOONS SEA SALT

2 TABLESPOONS HONEY OR MAPLE SYRUP

½ TEASPOON VANILLA EXTRACT, OR SEEDS FROM ½ VANILLA BEAN

2 TO 3 TEASPOONS GROUND CARDAMOM

1. Place the almonds, cashews, and sea salt in a food processor fitted with a metal S-shaped blade.
2. Process until the consistency is completely smooth, approximately 5 to 15 minutes depending on the power of the food processor's motor. If the nuts get stuck to the sides, pause the machine and use a rubber spatula to scrape them down as many times as needed. The nut butter is done when the texture is smooth and runny, the blade glides easily through the mixture, and there are no longer any chunks.

(CONTINUED)

GLUTEN-FREE + DAIRY-FREE + VEGAN OPTION + REFINED SUGAR-FREE + PALEO

3. Add the honey, vanilla, and 2 teaspoons of the cardamom. Process for an additional 1 to 3 minutes, or until the texture is again completely smooth and all ingredients are fully incorporated.
4. Taste it at this point, and add an additional teaspoon of cardamom, if desired, processing for an additional 30 seconds to thoroughly incorporate.
5. Transfer the mixture to two (8-ounce) glass jars. The nut butter will keep for 1 year without refrigeration. If the oils naturally separate over time, simply stir to incorporate.

Variation † LOVE CHAI? TURN THIS INTO A CHAI SPICED NUT BUTTER BY ADDING 2 TEASPOONS OF GROUND CINNAMON, ½ TEASPOON OF GROUND NUTMEG, AND ½ TEASPOON OF GROUND CLOVES IN STEP 3 OF THE ABOVE RECIPE.

Walnut–Cashew Butter

Makes 2 cups (16 ounces)

This nut butter is savory and rich, with a creamy nuttiness that reminds us of tahini. We find ourselves wanting to spread it on everything we eat, from savory eggplant dishes to chocolaty desserts. While walnut butter can be quite bitter on its own, the cashews lend a sweetness here that balances it out beautifully.

3 CUPS UNSALTED WALNUTS, TOASTED

2 CUPS UNSALTED CASHEWS, TOASTED

1 TEASPOON SEA SALT

1. Place the walnuts, cashews, and sea salt in a food processor fitted with an S-shaped metal blade.
2. Process until the consistency is completely smooth, approximately 5 to 10 minutes depending on the power of your food processor. If the nuts get stuck to the sides, pause the machine and use a rubber spatula to scrape them down as many times as needed. The nut butter is done when the texture is smooth and runny, the blade glides easily through the mixture, and there are no longer any chunks.
3. Transfer the mixture to two (8-ounce) glass jars. The nut butter will keep for 1 year without refrigeration. If the oils naturally separate over time, simply stir to incorporate.

GLUTEN-FREE + DAIRY-FREE + VEGAN + REFINED SUGAR-FREE + WHOLE30 + PALEO + KETO

Ground Up Espresso Stout Nut Butter

Makes 2 cups (16 ounces)

Our Espresso Stout flavor will take your mornings to an entirely new level of luxury. With a rich coffee flavor, this creamy nut butter is delicious stirred into oatmeal, enjoyed on pancakes, and served atop yogurt.

Despite the name, it has no relation to beer . . . but it does have a similarly toasty quality, and so we added "stout" to the name. We have sold it in limited-edition runs since we first got started, and customers are always asking us to bring it back for the long haul. And, who knows, perhaps one day we will! Until we do, here's how you can make your own.

2 CUPS UNSALTED ALMONDS, TOASTED

1 CUP UNSALTED CASHEWS, TOASTED

1½ CUP SHREDDED UNSWEETENED COCONUT, TOASTED

1 TEASPOON SEA SALT

2 TABLESPOONS HONEY OR MAPLE SYRUP

2 TABLESPOONS INSTANT ESPRESSO POWDER*

1 TEASPOON VANILLA EXTRACT, OR SEEDS FROM 1 VANILLA BEAN

1. Place the almonds, cashews, coconut, and sea salt in a food processor fitted with an S-shaped metal blade.
2. Process until the consistency is completely smooth, approximately 8 to 10 minutes depending on the power of the food processor's motor. If the nuts get stuck to the sides, pause the machine and use a rubber spatula to scrape them down as many times as needed. The nut butter is done when the blade glides easily through the mixture, and there are no longer any chunks.

GLUTEN-FREE + DAIRY-FREE + VEGAN OPTION + REFINED SUGAR-FREE + PALEO

3. Add the honey, espresso powder, and vanilla. Process for an additional 4 to 5 minutes, or until the texture is again completely smooth and all ingredients are fully incorporated.
4. Transfer the mixture to two (8-ounce) glass jars. The nut butter will keep for 1 year without refrigeration. If the oils naturally separate over time, simply stir to incorporate. If the nut butter hardens over time (due to the coconut), warm it by placing the jar in a bowl of hot water or by heating in the microwave for 15 seconds.

Note +

WE USE MEDAGLIA D'ORO ESPRESSO INSTANT COFFEE. IN OUR EXPERIENCE, GROUND COFFEE BEANS WON'T WORK HERE; THEY WON'T DISSOLVE!

Pumpkin Seed–Almond Butter

Makes 2½ cups (20 ounces)

We often get requests to add a seed butter to our lineup, and while we don't have plans to introduce one at this point, we wanted to include a recipe for you to make at home. We also couldn't help but add almonds to this, as well; it just tastes better, in our opinion! But you can also make it as a straight-up pumpkin seed butter—simply omit the almonds and ¼ teaspoon of the sea salt.

With its savory autumnal notes, we love to use this as a base for salad dressings and spread on toast in the morning. This will be a lot thicker than other nut butters, and it may take a while for the pumpkin seeds to turn to butter. But have faith and keep processing; it will get there!

3 CUPS UNSALTED PUMPKIN SEEDS, TOASTED

1 TEASPOON SEA SALT

1 CUP UNSALTED ALMONDS, TOASTED

2 TEASPOONS COCONUT OIL

1 TABLESPOON HONEY OR MAPLE SYRUP

¼ TEASPOON VANILLA EXTRACT, OR SEEDS FROM ¼ VANILLA BEAN

1. Place the pumpkin seeds and sea salt in a food processor fitted with an S-shaped metal blade.
2. Process until the consistency is completely smooth, approximately 10 to 15 minutes depending on the power of the food processor's motor. If the seeds get stuck to the sides, pause the machine and use a rubber spatula to scrape them down as many times as needed. The butter is done when the texture is no longer crumbly, the blade glides easily through the mixture, and no chunks remain.
3. Add the almonds and coconut oil. Process 4 to 6 minutes, or until smooth again, scraping down the sides as you go, if necessary.

GLUTEN-FREE + DAIRY-FREE + VEGAN OPTION + REFINED SUGAR-FREE + PALEO

4. Add the honey and vanilla. Process an additional 5 to 7 minutes, or until smooth again. At this point, you will have a butter that is quite thick and a bit textured, but it should be smooth overall.
5. Transfer the mixture to two (8-ounce) glass jars. The nut butter will keep for 1 year without refrigeration. If the oils naturally separate over time, simply stir to incorporate.

Ground Up Cinnamon Snickerdoodle Nut Butter

Makes 2 cups (16 ounces)

Our most popular flavor continues to be our Snickerdoodle. It could be because it's named after your grandma's favorite cookie . . . but it's actually healthy! Pair it with apples, and this nut butter will make you feel like you're sitting down to a warm piece of apple pie.

1½ CUPS UNSALTED ALMONDS, TOASTED

1½ CUPS UNSALTED CASHEWS, TOASTED

1½ CUPS SHREDDED UNSWEETENED COCONUT, TOASTED

½ TEASPOON SEA SALT

4 TEASPOONS GROUND CINNAMON

1 TABLESPOON HONEY

1 TEASPOON VANILLA EXTRACT, OR SEEDS FROM 1 VANILLA BEAN

1. Place the almonds, cashews, coconut, and sea salt in a food processor fitted with an S-shaped metal blade.
2. Process until the consistency is completely smooth, approximately 8 to 10 minutes depending on the power of your food processor. If the nuts get stuck to the sides, pause the machine and use a rubber spatula to scrape them down as many times as needed. The nut butter is done when the texture is smooth and runny, the blade glides easily through the mixture, and there are no longer any chunks.

GLUTEN-FREE + DAIRY-FREE + REFINED SUGAR-FREE + PALEO

3. Add the cinnamon, honey, and vanilla. Process for an additional 5 to 7 minutes, or until the texture is again completely smooth and all ingredients are fully incorporated.

4. Transfer the mixture to two (8-ounce) glass jars. The nut butter will keep for 1 year without refrigeration. If the oils naturally separate over time, simply stir to incorporate. If the nut butter hardens over time (due to the coconut), warm it by placing the jar in a bowl of hot water, or by heating in the microwave for 15 seconds.

Ground Up Oregon Hazelnut Butter

Makes 2 cups (16 ounces)

We're proud Oregon residents: Did you know that 99 percent of U.S. hazelnuts are grown in our state? This sweet and subtly spicy flavor highlights our favorite local crop. Made from a blend of almonds and hazelnuts, it's finished off with toasted hazelnuts for a chunky texture. We love to use this flavor in a gourmet NBJ (that's Nut Butter and Jelly!), or serve it alongside cheese, crackers, and charcuterie.

This recipe makes a chunky nut butter, so if you prefer it to be smoother, you can just leave out the last ½ cup of hazelnuts at the end.

1½ CUPS UNSALTED ALMONDS, TOASTED

2 CUPS UNSALTED HAZELNUTS, TOASTED, DIVIDED

¾ TEASPOON SEA SALT

2 TEASPOONS CHILI POWDER

1 TABLESPOON HONEY

1 TEASPOON VANILLA EXTRACT, OR SEEDS FROM 1 VANILLA BEAN

1. Place the almonds, 1½ cups of the hazelnuts, and the sea salt in a food processor fitted with an S-shaped metal blade.
2. Process until the consistency is completely smooth, approximately 5 to 10 minutes depending on the power of your food processor. If the nuts get stuck to the sides, pause the machine and use a rubber spatula to scrape them down as many times as needed. The nut butter is done when the texture is smooth and runny, the blade glides easily through the mixture, and there are no longer any chunks.
3. Add the chili powder, honey, and vanilla. Process an additional 2 to 3 minutes, or until the texture is smooth again.

GLUTEN-FREE + DAIRY-FREE + REFINED SUGAR-FREE + PALEO

4. Add the remaining ½ cup of hazelnuts and pulse for 5 to 10 seconds, until just incorporated but chunks of nuts remain.
5. Transfer the mixture to two (8-ounce) jars. The nut butter will keep for 1 year without refrigeration. If the oils naturally separate over time, simply stir to incorporate.

Chocolate-Hazelnut Cashew Butter

Makes 2 cups (16 ounces)

If you're looking for a nut butter to savor by the spoonful to keep by your desk for when that sweet tooth hits, look no further than our Chocolate-Hazelnut Cashew Butter.

As you'll notice with many of the spreads on the market, it is difficult to create a delicious and creamy chocolate nut butter without refined sugar. But after much experimenting, we have finally cracked the code. By adding cashews to the traditional chocolate-hazelnut pairing and combining two different natural sweeteners, we were able to achieve the perfect texture and sweetness.

We prefer dark chocolate, but if you'd like yours sweeter, simply add another tablespoon or two of coconut sugar.

2 CUPS UNSALTED CASHEWS, TOASTED

2 CUPS UNSALTED HAZELNUTS, TOASTED

¾ TEASPOON SEA SALT

½ TEASPOON VANILLA EXTRACT, OR SEEDS FROM ½ VANILLA BEAN

¼ CUP COCONUT SUGAR

2 TABLESPOONS MAPLE SYRUP

1 TABLESPOON COCONUT OIL, MELTED

½ CUP UNSWEETENED COCOA POWDER

¼ CUP CACAO NIBS, TOASTED (OPTIONAL)

1. Place the cashews, hazelnuts, and sea salt in a food processor fitted with an S-shaped metal blade.
2. Process until the consistency is completely smooth, approximately 5 to 10 minutes depending on the power of your food processor. If the nuts get stuck to the sides, pause the machine and use a rubber spatula to scrape them down as many times as needed. The nut butter is done when the texture is smooth and runny, the blade glides easily through the mixture, and there are no longer any chunks.

GLUTEN-FREE + DAIRY-FREE + VEGAN + REFINED SUGAR-FREE + PALEO

3. Add the vanilla, coconut sugar, maple syrup, coconut oil, and cocoa powder. Process an additional 3 to 5 minutes, or until smooth.

4. Add the cacao nibs if using, and pulse for 5 to 10 seconds, until just incorporated. (The cacao nibs add crunch and added flavor to each spoonful.)

5. Transfer the mixture to two (8-ounce) glass jars. The nut butter will keep for 1 year without refrigeration. If the oils naturally separate over time, simply stir to incorporate.

Pumpkin Spice Nut Butter

Makes 2 cups (16 ounces)

This almond-cashew butter is infused with sweet autumnal spices and swirled with chunks of pumpkin seeds and cranberries, making it the perfect nut butter for fall. We sold it back in the early days as "Harvest Spice" because we didn't want to come off as basic and call it what it really is: pumpkin spice latte in nut butter form.

1½ CUPS UNSALTED ALMONDS, TOASTED

1½ CUPS UNSALTED CASHEWS, TOASTED

¾ TEASPOON SEA SALT

2 TABLESPOONS MAPLE SYRUP

2 TEASPOONS GROUND CINNAMON

½ TEASPOON GROUND NUTMEG (OR ½ WHOLE NUTMEG, GRATED)

¼ TEASPOON GROUND ALLSPICE

½ TEASPOON GROUND GINGER

2 TEASPOONS VANILLA EXTRACT, OR SEEDS FROM 2 VANILLA BEANS

⅓ CUP UNSALTED PUMPKIN SEEDS, TOASTED

⅓ CUP DRIED UNSWEETENED CRANBERRIES

1. Place the almonds, cashews, and sea salt in a food processor fitted with an S-shaped metal blade.
2. Process until the consistency is completely smooth, approximately 5 to 15 minutes depending on the power of your food processor. If the nuts get stuck to the sides, pause the machine and use a rubber spatula to scrape them down as many times as needed. The nut butter is done when the texture is smooth and runny, the blade glides easily through the mixture, and there are no longer any chunks.
3. Add the maple syrup, cinnamon, nutmeg, allspice, ginger, and vanilla. Process for an additional 3 to 4 minutes, or until the texture is again completely smooth and all ingredients are fully incorporated.

GLUTEN-FREE + DAIRY-FREE + VEGAN + REFINED SUGAR-FREE + PALEO

4. Add in the pumpkin seeds and cranberries. Pulse for 5 to 10 seconds, until just incorporated and the texture remains chunky.
5. Transfer mixture to two (8-ounce) glass jars. The nut butter will keep for 1 year without refrigeration. If the oils naturally separate over time, simply stir to incorporate.

Ground Up Classic Smooth Nut Butter

Makes 2 cups (16 ounces)

Customers are always shocked to learn that this nut butter (the smooth counterpart to our Chunky Almond, Cashew + Coconut Butter flavor) is free of any added sweeteners. It just tastes too good to be true! We attribute its sweetness to the natural sugars in coconut and cashews. This nut butter is great on its own or as a base for different dressings and sauces, such as our Creamy Vegan "Alfredo" Sauce (page 108)!

2 CUPS UNSALTED ALMONDS, TOASTED

1½ CUPS UNSALTED CASHEWS, TOASTED

1 CUP SHREDDED UNSWEETENED COCONUT, TOASTED

1¼ TEASPOON SEA SALT

1 TEASPOON VANILLA EXTRACT, OR SEEDS FROM 1 VANILLA BEAN

1. Place the almonds, cashews, coconut, sea salt, and vanilla in a food processor fitted with an S-shaped metal blade.
2. Process until the consistency is completely smooth, approximately 8 to 10 minutes depending on the power of your food processor. If the nuts get stuck to the sides, pause the machine and use a rubber spatula to scrape them down as many times as needed. The nut butter is done when the texture is smooth and runny, the blade glides easily through the mixture, and there are no longer any chunks.
3. Transfer the mixture to two (8-ounce) glass jars. The nut butter will keep for 1 year without refrigeration. If the oils naturally separate over time, simply stir to incorporate. If the nut butter hardens over time (due to the coconut), warm it by placing the jar in a bowl of hot water or by heating in the microwave for 15 seconds.

GLUTEN-FREE + DAIRY-FREE + VEGAN + REFINED SUGAR-FREE + WHOLE30 + PALEO + KETO

CHAPTER FOUR:

Breakfast

For those of you who wake up with a sweet tooth (and even for those of you who don't), nut butters are a wonderful way to kick off your morning. They provide an amazing source of fuel for your day and can be used in tons of creative ways. We like to add them to oatmeal, smoothies, and more. And we think you'll be surprised by all the ways nut butters can spice up that first meal of the day!

Acai Breakfast Bowl

Serves 1

Beautifully styled acai bowls have become increasingly popular in the health-food world over the past few years, and their trendiness is justified. Acai berries are not only rich in antioxidants but also full of heart-healthy fats and fiber—keeping you satiated for longer. We like to keep frozen acai packets on hand for when we're feeling fancy. Although this recipe could not be simpler, there is something so fanciful about enjoying a bright-purple bowl decorated with fruit and drizzled with nut butter. Acai packets come in packs of four, so this recipe could easily be doubled or quadrupled. This bowl isn't very sweet, so feel free to add honey or maple syrup to taste. We especially enjoy topping this with our Hazelnut-Ginger Granola (page 66).

1 (14-OUNCE) PACKAGE FROZEN, UNSWEETENED ACAI

¼ CUP FROZEN BLUEBERRIES

1½ TABLESPOONS ALMOND BUTTER, DIVIDED (PAGE 44)

¾ CUP UNSWEETENED COCONUT MILK

1 MEDIUM BANANA, DIVIDED

⅛ CUP GRANOLA OF CHOICE

1. Place the frozen acai package under hot water for 5 seconds, then, using your hands, break the frozen acai puree into large chunks while still in the packaging.
2. Transfer the acai to a blender or small food processor, and add the frozen blueberries, 1 tablespoon of the almond butter, the coconut milk, and half of the banana. Blend approximately 1 to 2 minutes, or until smooth.
3. Meanwhile, thinly slice the remaining half of the banana.
4. Pour the blended mixture into a bowl. Top with the banana slices, granola, and the remaining ½ tablespoon of nut butter. Serve cold.

GLUTEN-FREE + DAIRY-FREE + VEGAN + REFINED SUGAR-FREE

Hazelnut-Ginger Granola

Makes 11 to 12 cups

This granola is bursting with ginger spice and a decadent amount of dried fruits, nuts, and seeds—this is what granola dreams are made of. We love the toasted crunch of hazelnuts in our Ground Up Oregon Hazelnut Butter (page 56) and wanted to build on it with a warming spice like ginger. Inspired by the flavors of the Northwest, we paired it with dried figs and currants.

This granola is the perfect salty and sweet topping for a morning smoothie or acai bowl, and it's also a wonderful way to highlight our nut butters. In fact, every Christmas, we bake several large batches and gift wrap them to share with our employees, friends, and families. Making this in the cooler winter months is such a treat; our kitchen gets all warm and fragrant from the toasted nuts and spices.

2 CUPS OLD-FASHIONED ROLLED OATS

2 CUPS RAW HAZELNUTS, COARSELY CHOPPED

2 CUPS RAW PUMPKIN SEEDS

1 CUP UNSWEETENED COCONUT FLAKES

⅓ CUP COCONUT OIL

⅓ CUP HONEY OR MAPLE SYRUP

½ CUP OREGON HAZELNUT BUTTER (PAGE 56)

1 TEASPOON VANILLA EXTRACT, OR SEEDS FROM ½ VANILLA BEAN

2 TEASPOONS GROUND GINGER

2 TEASPOONS GROUND CINNAMON

¾ TEASPOON SEA SALT

1 CUP CRYSTALLIZED GINGER

½ CUP DRIED FIGS

1 CUP DRIED CURRANTS

GLUTEN-FREE + DAIRY-FREE + VEGAN OPTION

1. Preheat the oven to 325°F. Line a baking sheet with parchment paper.
2. In a large mixing bowl, combine the oats, hazelnuts, pumpkin seeds, and coconut flakes. Set aside.
3. In a small saucepan over low heat, melt the coconut oil and honey. Whisk in the nut butter, vanilla, ginger, cinnamon, and sea salt.
4. Remove the saucepan from the heat and pour the mixture into the bowl of dry ingredients. Use a wooden spoon to mix until completely combined.
5. Using a metal spatula, spread out the granola mixture evenly across the baking sheet, flattening the mixture into the edges of the pan to ensure good clusters.
6. Bake the granola for 10 minutes, then use a metal spatula to stir.
7. Bake for an additional 7 to 8 minutes, or until golden brown and the top has started to darken. Remove the granola from the oven.
8. Allow the mixture to cool for at least 1 hour.
9. Meanwhile, coarsely chop the crystallized ginger and dried figs.
10. Once the granola has cooled and hardened, use your hands to break it up into clusters. Transfer the clusters to a large bowl, and mix with the chopped crystallized ginger and figs and the currants until evenly distributed.
11. Transfer to glass jars and store in a cool, dry place for up to 1 month.

Note + WE INCLUDE CRYSTALLIZED GINGER IN THIS RECIPE, WHICH DOES CONTAIN SUGAR. WE FEEL IT'S A WORTHWHILE INDULGENCE IN THIS RECIPE, BUT YOU'RE WELCOME TO OMIT IT AND ADD A DRIED FRUIT INSTEAD.

Maple Walnut Spice Oatmeal

Serves 2

When customers ask us how we use our nut butters, Carolyn's answer is always that she stirs a spoonful into her morning oatmeal, telling them that "It's all the flavor you need!" And while it's certainly true that, at its simplest, you could cook up oats, stir in nut butter, and have a delicious breakfast, we couldn't resist going all out. This fall-spiced oatmeal will heat you up on a cold morning and impress breakfast guests on a special occasion. Notes of cinnamon and maple pair beautifully with the fresh figs and walnuts. If you aren't able to catch fresh figs during their short, sweet season, we suggest opting for fresh raspberries or dried figs instead. You could also replace the oats with another grain, such as quinoa, buckwheat, or amaranth.

1 CUP OLD-FASHIONED ROLLED OATS

1 CUP UNSWEETENED ALMOND OR COCONUT MILK

1 CUP WATER

½ TEASPOON SEA SALT

3 TABLESPOONS DRIED CURRANTS

3 TABLESPOONS HEMP SEEDS

1 TEASPOON GROUND CINNAMON

¼ TEASPOON GROUND ALLSPICE

¼ TEASPOON GROUND GINGER

½ TEASPOON VANILLA EXTRACT, OR SEEDS FROM ½ VANILLA BEAN

6 FRESH OR DRIED FIGS

⅓ CUP WALNUTS, TOASTED

4 TEASPOONS MAPLE SYRUP

2 TABLESPOONS WALNUT-CASHEW BUTTER (PAGE 49)

GLUTEN-FREE + DAIRY-FREE + VEGAN + REFINED SUGAR-FREE

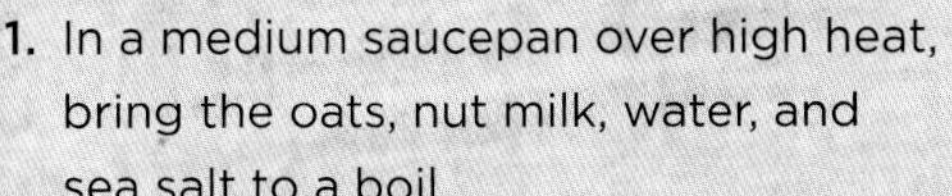

1. In a medium saucepan over high heat, bring the oats, nut milk, water, and sea salt to a boil.
2. Decrease the heat to medium and gently stir in the currants, hemp seeds, cinnamon, allspice, ginger, and vanilla.
3. Cover the saucepan and simmer for 8 to 10 minutes, until the oats are fully cooked but some liquid remains.
4. Meanwhile, thinly slice the figs and coarse chop the walnuts.
5. Remove the oatmeal from the heat and divide between two bowls.
6. Drizzle each bowl with 2 teaspoons of maple syrup and 1 tablespoon of the nut butter. Sprinkle with the chopped walnuts and figs. Serve warm.

Coconut Crêpes with Chocolate-Hazelnut Cashew Butter

Makes 6 (7-inch) crêpes

If you have company spending the night and you are looking for an easy, yet impressive, brunch, these crêpes are a sure winner. Paleo and grain-free, they are sweetened with a touch of honey and infused with flavors of coconut and cinnamon. We love to top them with our chocolate nut butter, homemade coconut cream, and fruit, but any nut butter or topping would be delicious. It's also fun to set out a few different toppings for guests to mix and match.

The crêpes can be quite fragile, so be gentle with them. We recommend adding a sprinkle of flaky sea salt on them as they're cooking for an extra hint of salt in each bite!

5 MEDIUM EGGS

½ TEASPOON ALMOND EXTRACT

1 TABLESPOON COCONUT OIL, MELTED, PLUS EXTRA TO GREASE THE PAN

⅓ CUP UNSWEETENED ALMOND MILK

2 TABLESPOONS HONEY

6 TABLESPOONS COCONUT FLOUR

1 TEASPOON GROUND CINNAMON

½ TEASPOON SEA SALT

¼ CUP CHOCOLATE-HAZELNUT CASHEW BUTTER (PAGE 58)

1 MEDIUM BANANA, SLICED INTO ¼-INCH-THICK SLICES

1 CUP FRESH STRAWBERRIES, SLICED (OR ¼ CUP STRAWBERRY JAM IF BERRIES ARE OUT OF SEASON)

1 CUP COCONUT CREAM (SEE RECIPE AT RIGHT) OR YOGURT OF CHOICE, FOR GARNISH

2 TABLESPOONS CACAO NIBS, TOASTED, FOR GARNISH

GLUTEN-FREE + DAIRY-FREE + REFINED SUGAR-FREE + PALEO

1. In a large bowl, whisk the eggs, almond extract, coconut oil, almond milk, and honey together until fully incorporated.
2. Add the coconut flour, cinnamon, and sea salt, and mix until fully incorporated.
3. Heat a medium-size skillet (at least 10 inches in diameter) to medium-high heat.
4. Add enough coconut oil to thinly coat the bottom of the pan.
5. Once the pan is hot, scoop ⅓ cup of the batter onto the skillet, and gently swirl the pan to spread out the batter evenly. (The crêpes should be quite thin; no more than ¼-inch thick.)
6. Cook until bubbles form on the surface of the crêpe and the ends begin to curl up, approximately 2 to 3 minutes. Using your fingers instead of a spatula, gently flip the crêpe, and cook for an additional 30 seconds to 1 minute.
7. Carefully transfer the crêpe to a plate, again using your fingers if that is easier than a spatula, and repeat until all of the batter is used up.
8. Spread each crêpe with 1 tablespoon of the nut butter, then top with the sliced banana, berries, coconut cream, and a sprinkle of cacao nibs.
9. Serve warm, either rolled up or as open crêpes. If you have leftover crêpes, they will keep refrigerated for up to 2 days.

To Make Coconut Cream † CHILL 1 (14-OUNCE) CAN OF FULL-FAT COCONUT MILK OVERNIGHT, OR FOR AT LEAST 8 HOURS. SCOOP THE SOLID CREAM PART INTO A LARGE MIXING BOWL (RESERVING THE REMAINING LIQUID FOR ANOTHER USE), AND COMBINE WITH 1 TABLESPOON OF HONEY, 1 TEASPOON OF VANILLA, AND ⅛ TEASPOON OF SEA SALT. MIX ON HIGH UNTIL LIGHT AND FLUFFY, APPROXIMATELY 1 MINUTE.

Cardamom Kick-Start Smoothie

Serves 1

Most mornings you'll find us bustling into our warehouse, balancing a smoothie in one hand and boxes of product or supplies in the other. We both love to start our days with a smoothie. Not only does it energize us for the busy day to come but also it couldn't be easier to whip together in the morning as we are running out the door.

When we decided to write this cookbook, we were certain that we would include at least one smoothie recipe . . . but we thought narrowing it down to just one would be next to impossible. However, once we began discussing it, we realized that, unknown to each other, we had been making *the same exact* smoothie every morning: a banana, mango, and spinach smoothie with our cardamom nut butter. It's tasty, uncomplicated, and made with our favorite nut butter flavor, so we shouldn't have been surprised by the coincidence.

We love to sprinkle some granola in it and eat it with a spoon . . . when we have the time to sit down, that is. If you're into floral flavors, this recipe is also delicious with our Ground Up Lavender Honey Nut Butter, which you can purchase.

1 MEDIUM BANANA

1½ TABLESPOONS CARDAMOM ALMOND–CASHEW BUTTER (PAGE 47)

⅓ CUP FROZEN MANGO CHUNKS

½ CUP LOOSELY PACKED SPINACH

¾ CUP UNSWEETENED ALMOND MILK

½ TEASPOON LEMON ZEST (OPTIONAL)

1. In a blender, combine the banana, nut butter, mango, spinach, almond milk, and lemon zest if using, until smooth. If the resulting mixture is too thick, add ¼ cup of water or additional almond milk. Enjoy!

GLUTEN-FREE + DAIRY-FREE + VEGAN OPTION + REFINED SUGAR-FREE + PALEO

Harvest Overnight Oats

Serves 1

This single-serving breakfast is our go-to on mornings when we're working the local farmers' market. It's easy to prep the night before and grab on the way out the door. Once we've hustled to set our booth up, we'll mix a spoonful of nut butter into the oats, and enjoy it before the market is underway. We savor those quiet moments on cool, crisp market mornings before the crowds come. It's nice to take a moment to appreciate the bounty of local produce and artisanal goods, catch up with other vendors, and savor a simple but hearty breakfast. We know you'll love this recipe for your busy mornings, too!

½ CUP OLD-FASHIONED ROLLED OATS

1 TABLESPOON CHIA SEEDS

⅔ CUP UNSWEETENED ALMOND MILK

1 TABLESPOON GROUND FLAXSEED MEAL (OPTIONAL)

½ TEASPOON GROUND CINNAMON

¼ TEASPOON VANILLA EXTRACT, OR SEEDS FROM ¼ VANILLA BEAN

¼ TEASPOON SEA SALT

1 TEASPOON MAPLE SYRUP

½ BANANA, SLICED

1 TABLESPOON PUMPKIN SPICE NUT BUTTER (PAGE 60)

1 TABLESPOON DRIED CURRANTS

1 TABLESPOON PUMPKIN SEEDS, TOASTED

1. Combine the oats, chia seeds, almond milk, flaxseed meal if using, the cinnamon, vanilla, and sea salt in a 12- or 16-ounce glass jar. Shake the oat mixture to combine.
2. Place the jar in the refrigerator overnight, or for at least 8 hours.
3. Remove the oatmeal from the refrigerator and stir in the maple syrup.
4. Top with the banana, nut butter, currants, and pumpkin seeds.
5. The oat mixture will keep for up to 3 days in the refrigerator.

GLUTEN-FREE + DAIRY-FREE + VEGAN + REFINED SUGAR-FREE

Mocha Chia Pudding Parfait

Serves 4

Decadent enough to be a dessert, this chia pudding parfait is perfect for anyone who wakes up with a sweet tooth in the morning (ahem . . . Carolyn). With layers of mocha chia pudding, vanilla yogurt, Espresso Stout Nut Butter, and banana slices, it's not only beautiful but sure to keep you buzzing (in the best way!) all day long.

2 TABLESPOONS INSTANT COFFEE GRANULES

2 TABLESPOONS BOILING WATER

⅔ CUP CHIA SEEDS

2 CUPS UNSWEETENED ALMOND MILK

2 TABLESPOONS UNSWEETENED COCOA POWDER

½ TEASPOON VANILLA EXTRACT, OR SEEDS FROM ½ VANILLA BEAN

½ TEASPOON SEA SALT

¼ CUP AND 4 TEASPOONS PURE MAPLE SYRUP, DIVIDED

4 MEDIUM BANANAS, SLICED

¼ CUP ESPRESSO STOUT NUT BUTTER (PAGE 50)

1 CUP DAIRY-FREE VANILLA YOGURT, DIVIDED

¼ CUP CACAO NIBS, TOASTED, DIVIDED, FOR GARNISH

1. In a medium bowl, mix the instant coffee with the boiling water, stirring until dissolved.
2. Add the chia seeds, almond milk, cocoa powder, vanilla, sea salt, and the ¼ cup of maple syrup.
3. Stir the mixture to combine, then cover with plastic wrap and leave out at room temperature overnight. (You could also keep it in the refrigerator overnight—especially if it is a hot summer day—but we enjoy it more when it is not super cold in the morning.)
4. Divide half of the chia mixture between four parfait glasses or bowls. Evenly layer half of the sliced bananas, ½ tablespoon each of Espresso Stout Nut Butter, half the yogurt, and half the cacao nibs.

(CONTINUED)

GLUTEN-FREE + DAIRY-FREE + VEGAN OPTION + REFINED SUGAR-FREE + PALEO

5. Evenly top each parfait with the remaining chia mixture. Garnish each parfait with 1 teaspoon of the maple syrup, the remaining nut butter and remaining banana slices.
6. Top with the remaining yogurt and the remaining cacao nibs. Serve at room temperature, or the parfaits can be refrigerated for up to 1 week.

Note † SINCE THESE PARFAITS KEEP EASILY IN THE REFRIGERATOR FOR UP TO A WEEK, WE SUGGEST PREPPING AT THE BEGINNING OF THE WEEK IN INDIVIDUAL GLASS JARS (OUR 12-OUNCE GROUND UP GLASS JARS WORK PERFECTLY HERE!), SO THAT IT'S EASY TO GRAB AND GO EACH MORNING.

Cardamom Banana Bread with Nut Butter Streusel

Makes 1 (9 by 5-inch) loaf

This gluten-free banana bread is insanely moist and full of flavor. It is one of the first baked goods we ever made with our nut butters, and we immediately printed the recipe on cute recipe cards that would go out with every customer's order. I am still astounded by the number of people who have emailed or reached out to say that they made this recipe and it was the best banana bread they'd ever had. We think it's the cardamom nut butter streusel that sets it apart—but we'll let you decide for yourself!

¼ CUP COCONUT OIL, PLUS EXTRA TO GREASE THE PAN

4 EGGS

3 MEDIUM-SIZE RIPE BANANAS

½ TEASPOON VANILLA EXTRACT, OR SEEDS FROM ½ VANILLA BEAN

¾ CUP CARDAMOM ALMOND-CASHEW BUTTER, DIVIDED (PAGE 47)

⅜ CUP COCONUT SUGAR, DIVIDED

½ CUP COCONUT FLOUR

½ TEASPOON BAKING SODA

½ TEASPOON BAKING POWDER

½ TEASPOON SEA SALT

¾ CUP OLD-FASHIONED ROLLED OATS, DIVIDED

1. Preheat the oven to 350°F. Grease a 9 by 5-inch loaf pan with coconut oil.
2. In a large mixing bowl, whisk the eggs.
3. Add the bananas and mash with a fork, or use a hand mixer to incorporate.
4. Melt the coconut oil in the microwave on high for 15 seconds, if it's not already liquid at room temperature. Add to the mixing bowl, along with the vanilla, ¼ cup of the nut butter, and ¼ cup of the coconut sugar.
5. Beat on high for 2 to 3 minutes, or mix by hand, until all the ingredients are fully incorporated.
6. Stir in the coconut flour, baking soda, baking powder, sea salt, and ½ cup of the oats.

(CONTINUED)

GLUTEN-FREE + DAIRY-FREE + REFINED SUGAR-FREE

7. Transfer to the prepared loaf pan.
8. Make a streusel using the remaining ⅛ cup of coconut sugar, the remaining ¼ cup of oats, and the remaining ½ cup of nut butter. Stir all of the ingredients together and sprinkle over the top of the batter.
9. Cover with aluminum foil and bake for 50 to 55 minutes until brown, or until a toothpick inserted comes out clean. Allow to cool completely. Store in an airtight container for up to 5 days.

Note † IF YOU'D PREFER, YOU CAN SUBSTITUTE ALL-PURPOSE FLOUR FOR THE COCONUT FLOUR, AND IT'LL STILL TASTE GREAT.

Oatmeal-Banana Breakfast Cookies

Makes 18 to 20 large cookies

You may have noticed that we are *very* into breakfasts that require minimal effort—but that still taste delicious and will fuel us for our busy days. Filled with banana, egg, oats, nuts, seeds, and dried fruits, we think it's basically the healthiest way you could start your day.

Now, in case you haven't yet been introduced to the wonder that is the breakfast cookie, let us fill you in. Breakfast cookies are filled with healthy fats, free of refined sugar, and essentially a healthy meal replacement for breakfast on the go. We recommend baking up a batch at the beginning of the week and enjoying them all week long.

This recipe is a fun one to play around with—feel free to swap out the nut butter (the Pumpkin Spice, for instance, is also quite good here), and change up the fruits and nuts that you add in. Texturally, these cookies are a mix between banana bread and an oatmeal cookie—they're the perfect treat for enjoying with your morning tea or coffee.

1 MEDIUM BANANA

1 EGG

¼ CUP COCONUT OIL, MELTED

2 TABLESPOONS MAPLE SYRUP

½ CUP PUMPKIN SEED-ALMOND BUTTER (PAGE 52)

½ TEASPOON SEA SALT

1 TEASPOON GROUND CINNAMON

¼ TEASPOON BAKING SODA

½ CUP OAT FLOUR

1 CUP OLD-FASHIONED ROLLED OATS

⅓ CUP RAW WALNUTS, COARSELY CHOPPED

⅓ CUP RAW PUMPKIN SEEDS

¼ CUP SHREDDED, UNSWEETENED COCONUT

⅓ CUP DRIED FRUIT (E.G., CURRANTS OR GOJI BERRIES)

⅛ CUP CACAO NIBS (OPTIONAL)

(CONTINUED)

GLUTEN-FREE + DAIRY-FREE + REFINED SUGAR-FREE

1. Preheat the oven to 350°F. Line a baking sheet with parchment paper.
2. In a large mixing bowl, mash the banana with a fork.
3. Add the egg, coconut oil, maple syrup, and nut butter. Whisk together until well-combined.
4. Use a wooden spoon to mix in the sea salt, cinnamon, baking soda, oat flour, and rolled oats until well-combined.
5. Fold in the walnuts, pumpkin seeds, coconut, dried fruit, and cacao nibs if using.
6. Using a 2-tablespoon scoop, drop the cookie mixture onto the prepared baking sheet.
7. Bake cookies for 8 to 9 minutes, or until the tops have set. Remove from the oven and allow to cool for at least 5 minutes.
8. Store cookies at room temperature for up to 1 week, or freeze for up to 6 months.

Nut Butter Mocha Latte

Serves 1

Anyone who has met Julie would be surprised to learn that she is not a coffee drinker. (It's astounding that so much natural energy can be found in a single human, we know.) But for Carolyn and the rest of us out there in need of their morning caffeine fix, this latte situation is a real game changer. Adding nut butter to your standard latte not only makes it unbelievably creamy but also provides healthy fats to kick-start your morning. Moreover, it's so luxurious that you won't even miss the whole-milk latte.

We recommend using a mini blender like the Magic Bullet for this, as it ensures the smoothest consistency. If you don't have one, you could heat the nut butter in a microwave on high power for 15 seconds, and then whisk it together with the other ingredients.

1 CUP HOT, STRONG COFFEE

1 TABLESPOON CLASSIC SMOOTH NUT BUTTER (PAGE 62)

1½ TEASPOONS UNSWEETENED COCOA POWDER

¼ CUP UNSWEETENED ALMOND MILK

1½ TEASPOONS MAPLE SYRUP OR HONEY

¼ TEASPOON CINNAMON, PLUS EXTRA FOR GARNISH

¼ TEASPOON ALMOND EXTRACT

1. Combine the coffee, nut butter, cocoa powder, almond milk, maple syrup, cinnamon, and almond extract in a small blender and process until smooth, approximately 1 minute.
2. Transfer latte to a mug and finish with a sprinkle of cinnamon. Serve immediately.

GLUTEN-FREE + DAIRY-FREE + VEGAN + REFINED SUGAR-FREE + PALEO

Paleo Pumpkin Pancakes

Makes 10 (4-inch) pancakes

These grain-free pancakes are a delicious way to start the day, particularly if you are fueling up for an autumnal adventure. Loaded with our Cinnamon Snickerdoodle Nut Butter and spiced with nutmeg, clove, and allspice, these pumpkin pancakes will give you all the fall feels. The best part? While the average pancake leaves you hungry two hours later, these protein-packed babies will keep you feeling satisfied for the entire morning.

½ CUP CANNED PUMPKIN PUREE

½ CUP CINNAMON SNICKERDOODLE NUT BUTTER (PAGE 54)

4 EGGS

2 TEASPOONS BAKING POWDER

½ TEASPOON SEA SALT

¼ TEASPOON GROUND CLOVE

¼ TEASPOON GROUND NUTMEG (OR ⅛ WHOLE NUTMEG, GRATED)

¼ TEASPOON GROUND ALLSPICE

½ CUP ALMOND MEAL

¼ CUP COCONUT SUGAR

¼ CUP COCONUT OIL

2 TABLESPOONS MAPLE SYRUP

1 CUP DAIRY-FREE COCONUT YOGURT

¼ CUP PUMPKIN SEEDS, TOASTED

¼ CUP DRIED CRANBERRIES

DARK CHOCOLATE CHIPS (OPTIONAL)

(CONTINUED)

GLUTEN-FREE + DAIRY-FREE + REFINED SUGAR-FREE + PALEO

1. In a large mixing bowl, combine the pumpkin puree, nut butter, eggs, baking powder, sea salt, clove, nutmeg, allspice, almond meal, and coconut sugar. Mix until fully incorporated, approximately 2 to 3 minutes.
2. Heat a medium skillet over medium heat, and add coconut oil, melting to coat the bottom.
3. When the skillet is hot and the oil begins to sizzle, add a ⅓ cup scoop of the pancake mix. (The pancakes should be no wider than 4 inches in diameter or they may fall apart when you try to flip them with a spatula.)
4. Cook the pancakes for 4 to 5 minutes, or until bubbles form on the top. Using a metal spatula, flip the pancakes and cook for an additional minute, then transfer to a plate. Repeat the process with the remaining batter.
5. Serve the pancakes with the maple syrup, coconut yogurt, pumpkin seeds, dried cranberries, and the dark chocolate chips if using.

Note † **IF YOU *REALLY* WANT TO TREAT YOURSELF, JULIE RECOMMENDS ADDING DARK CHOCOLATE CHIPS FOR A DECADENT START TO THE DAY**

CHAPTER FIVE:

Snacks + Bites

While nut butter and fruit makes for an easy and delicious snack on the go, there are so many other ways to incorporate nut butters into your snacking routine. They're a great way to get that afternoon energy boost or fuel yourself before or after a workout. Here, we're sharing some of our favorite ways to use nut butters as a midday pick-me-up.

Cardamom Granola "Bar-nies"

Makes 16 (1 by 2-inch) bars

Someone who tried these granola bars once dubbed them "bar-nies," and the name has stuck. We think it is the perfect way to describe this blend between a granola bar and a blondie—a sweet treat that is also healthy. They serve as a substitute for breakfast, as an on-the-go snack, or as a delicious dessert. We often bake up a few batches of these bars to sell or sample at events, and customers have told us that these were the best granola bars they'd ever tasted. We agree.

1½ CUPS OLD-FASHIONED ROLLED OATS

½ CUP RAW ALMONDS, COARSELY CHOPPED

½ CUP RAW CASHEW PIECES

1 CUP SHREDDED, UNSWEETENED COCONUT

1 TEASPOON GROUND CARDAMOM

2 TABLESPOONS COCONUT OIL

1 CUP CARDAMOM ALMOND-CASHEW BUTTER (PAGE 47)

⅓ CUP HONEY

1 TEASPOON ALMOND EXTRACT

½ TEASPOON SEA SALT

½ CUP DARK CHOCOLATE CHIPS

1. Preheat the oven to 350°F. Line a 9 by 13-inch baking sheet with parchment paper.
2. In a large mixing bowl, combine the oats, almonds, cashews, coconut, and cardamom.
3. In a small saucepan over low heat, melt the coconut oil. Whisk in the nut butter, honey, almond extract, and sea salt until smooth. The mixture will be quite thick.
4. Combine the liquid mixture with the dry mixture in the mixing bowl. Use a wooden spoon to stir together until incorporated. (It will be a thick, doughy texture and somewhat hard to mix.) Stir in the chocolate chips.
5. Transfer to the baking sheet and use a metal spatula to flatten the dough until evenly distributed.

GLUTEN-FREE + DAIRY-FREE + VEGAN OPTION

6. Bake for 10 minutes. Remove the pan from the oven and transfer to the refrigerator. Let it cool for at least 1 hour, preferably overnight.
7. Remove from the refrigerator, and cut into sixteen (1 by 2-inch) bars. Store at room temperature; they will last for up to 1 week. Or individually wrap and freeze for grabbing on the go!

Variation † THIS RECIPE HAS A STRONG ALMOND AND CARDAMOM FLAVOR; BUT IF THAT'S NOT YOUR JAM, FEEL FREE TO SWAP OUT THE ALMOND EXTRACT FOR VANILLA, OMIT THE CARDAMOM, AND SUBSTITUTE WITH ANOTHER NUT BUTTER INSTEAD.

Cinnamon-Date Chia Bars

Makes 15 (1½ by 2½-inch) bars

If we ever have a batch of nut butter that goes slightly wrong, or if we make extra, we immediately use it to whip up a batch of these babies. Inspired by our favorite snack bar, these homemade "Caro bars" (as our friends call them!) are great for on-the-go snacking. We'll bring a batch with us when we're heading out biking or camping for the weekend. Feel free to swap out different nut butters and dried fruits as a base, but we've found that you can't go wrong with this simple date and cinnamon combo!

1 CUP RAW ALMONDS

2 CUPS PITTED MEDJOOL DATES (APPROXIMATELY 35 DATES)

¾ CUP CINNAMON SNICKERDOODLE NUT BUTTER (PAGE 54)

2 TABLESPOONS CHIA SEEDS

1½ TABLESPOONS GROUND CINNAMON

¾ TEASPOON SEA SALT

1 TO 2 TEASPOONS COCONUT OIL (OPTIONAL)

¼ CUP CACAO NIBS, TOASTED (OPTIONAL)

1. In a food processor fitted with an S-shaped metal blade, combine the almonds, dates, nut butter, chia seeds, cinnamon, and sea salt. Process until a thick paste forms, approximately 2 to 3 minutes. The mixture should be oily rather than crumbly. (You should be able to see a bit of oil forming on the top of the dough.)
2. The moisture content may vary based on the freshness of the dates, so if yours are a bit dry, add 1 to 2 teaspoons of coconut oil and process for an additional 30 seconds to 1 minute, until fully incorporated or until it reaches a smooth, paste-like consistency.
3. Add the cacao nibs if using, and pulse quickly for 5 to 10 seconds, or until just incorporated.

GLUTEN-FREE + DAIRY-FREE + VEGAN OPTION + REFINED SUGAR-FREE + PALEO

4. Line an 8 by 8-inch baking sheet with waxed paper. Remove the date mixture from the food processor and spread out across the bottom of the pan.
5. Using a second piece of waxed paper, press the mixture down firmly into the pan so that it lines the bottom and is approximately ½-inch thick.
6. Transfer the pan to the refrigerator for at least 2 hours.
7. Remove from the refrigerator and use a serrated knife to slice into fifteen bars. Each bar should be around 1½ by 2½ inches long.
8. Wrap the bars individually in waxed paper for an easy, on-the-go snack, or transfer to an airtight container. They will last in the refrigerator for up to 3 weeks or in the freezer for up to 3 months.

Clockwise from top left: Banana Bread–Chocolate Chip Bliss Balls, Dark Chocolate–Hazelnut Bliss Balls, Pumpkin Spice Bliss Balls

Bliss Balls, Three Ways

We aren't sure when or where the trend for these no-bake, protein-packed "bliss balls" first began, but we do know that we hopped right on board. Bliss balls, sometimes called "energy bites" or "fat balls," are a favorite of ours when we need healthy fuel in a hurry—whether on a hiking adventure, in the midst of a busy workday, or as pre-workout nourishment. Here, we're sharing three of our favorite recipes, but we encourage you to play around and make up your own combination. Get creative; you really can't go wrong.

Note + THESE SHOULD BE MADE IN A FULL-SIZE FOOD PROCESSOR; A MINI BLENDER WON'T CUT IT HERE.

Pumpkin Spice Bliss Balls

Makes 14 balls

Rolled in coconut, these bites have the texture of cookie dough and the flavors of autumn. Really, what more could you want?

½ CUP PUMPKIN SPICE NUT BUTTER (PAGE 60)

¼ CUP OAT FLOUR

½ CUP OLD-FASHIONED ROLLED OATS

2 TABLESPOONS MAPLE SYRUP

½ CUP PITTED MEDJOOL DATES (8 TO 10 LARGE DATES)

¼ CUP RAW, SHELLED PUMPKIN SEEDS

2 TABLESPOONS UNSWEETENED ALMOND MILK

½ TEASPOON VANILLA EXTRACT, OR SEEDS FROM ½ VANILLA BEAN

¼ TEASPOON SEA SALT

⅓ CUP SHREDDED, UNSWEETENED COCONUT, FOR GARNISH

1. In a food processor fitted with an S-shaped metal blade, combine the nut butter, oat flour, rolled oats, maple syrup, dates, pumpkin seeds, almond milk, vanilla, and sea salt. Pulse until a sticky dough is formed, approximately 30 seconds to 1 minute.
2. Roll the dough into 1½-inch balls. Roll each ball in the coconut.
3. Transfer bites to the refrigerator for storage. They will keep for up to 2 weeks in the refrigerator or for up to 2 months in the freezer.

GLUTEN-FREE + DAIRY-FREE + VEGAN + REFINED SUGAR-FREE

Dark Chocolate–Hazelnut Bliss Balls

Makes 15 balls

The most decadent of the three recipes, these combine all of our favorite things: dark chocolate, toasted hazelnuts, and sweet dates. Make these when you really want a brownie; we promise they will do the trick.

¼ CUP OREGON HAZELNUT BUTTER (PAGE 56)

½ CUP OLD-FASHIONED ROLLED OATS

1 TABLESPOON HONEY

½ CUP PITTED MEDJOOL DATES (8 TO 10 LARGE DATES)

1 CUP HAZELNUTS, TOASTED

½ CUP WALNUTS, TOASTED

¼ CUP UNSWEETENED COCOA POWDER, DIVIDED

¼ TEASPOON SEA SALT

1. In a food processor fitted with an S-shaped metal blade, combine the nut butter, rolled oats, honey, dates, hazelnuts, walnuts, 3 tablespoons of the cocoa powder, and the sea salt. Pulse until a sticky dough is formed, approximately 30 seconds to 1 minute.
2. Roll the dough into 1½-inch balls. Roll each ball in the remaining cocoa powder.
3. Transfer the bites to the refrigerator for storage. They will keep for up to 2 weeks in the refrigerator or for up to 2 months in the freezer.

GLUTEN-FREE + DAIRY-FREE + REFINED SUGAR-FREE

Banana Bread–Chocolate Chip Bliss Balls

Makes 15 balls

We love the combination of banana, coconut, and dark chocolate in these bites. The best part? They pretty much taste like you're eating a scoop of chocolate chip cookie dough, and who doesn't love that?

6 TABLESPOONS CINNAMON SNICKERDOODLE NUT BUTTER (PAGE 54)

1 MEDIUM RIPE BANANA

1 CUP SHREDDED, UNSWEETENED COCONUT

2 TABLESPOONS CHIA SEEDS

¼ CUP COCONUT FLOUR

1 TABLESPOON MAPLE SYRUP

½ TEASPOON VANILLA EXTRACT, OR SEEDS FROM ½ VANILLA BEAN

¼ TEASPOON SEA SALT

¼ CUP DARK CHOCOLATE CHIPS

1. In a food processor fitted with an S-shaped metal blade, combine the nut butter, banana, coconut, chia seeds, coconut flour, maple syrup, vanilla, and sea salt. Pulse until a sticky dough forms, approximately 1 to 2 minutes. Add the chocolate chips and quickly pulse to incorporate, no more than 30 seconds.
2. Roll the dough into 1½-inch balls.
3. Transfer the bites to the refrigerator for storage. They will keep for up to 2 weeks in the refrigerator or for up to 2 months in the freezer.

GLUTEN-FREE + DAIRY-FREE + VEGAN OPTION

Stuffed Dates, Two Ways

Dates stuffed with nut butter are easily one of our favorite "party tricks." They always impress guests and could not be simpler to make. They highlight the flavors of our nut butters beautifully; in fact, we often recommend that stores sample our nut butters inside dates because it is such a healthy and delicious snack. Here, we're including two of our favorite pairings, one savory (which makes a great appetizer) and one sweet (for a simple dessert). Feel free to get creative with these, as well—try out different nut butters and toppings; they're great with everything from a slice of sharp cheese to a drizzle of honey.

Sweet: Cacao + Rose Petal

Makes 12 dates

If you want to play up the floral notes here, try our Ground Up Lavender Honey Nut Butter, which you can purchase. Dried rose petals can be found in many health food stores and select grocery stores, typically in the bulk herbs and teas section.

12 PITTED MEDJOOL DATES

¼ CUP CHOCOLATE-HAZELNUT CASHEW BUTTER (PAGE 58)

UNSWEETENED COCOA POWDER, FOR DUSTING

2 TABLESPOONS CACAO NIBS, TOASTED, FOR GARNISH

1 TABLESPOON DRIED ROSE PETALS, FOR GARNISH

1. Slice the dates lengthwise with a sharp knife, making sure not to cut all the way through.
2. Spoon 1 teaspoon of the nut butter inside each date.
3. Sprinkle each date with cocoa powder, sprinkle with cacao nibs and rose petals.
4. These can be made ahead and stored in an airtight container for up to 5 days.

GLUTEN-FREE + DAIRY-FREE + VEGAN + REFINED SUGAR-FREE + PALEO

Clockwise from top left: Sweet: Cacao + Rose Petal, Savory: Hazelnut + Prosciutto

Savory: Hazelnut + Prosciutto

Makes 12 dates

We love this gourmet twist on the classic bacon-wrapped date recipe; lightly crisped prosciutto pairs beautifully with the toasted hazelnut flavor!

12 PITTED MEDJOOL DATES

¼ CUP OREGON HAZELNUT BUTTER (PAGE 56)

GROUND CAYENNE PEPPER, FOR DUSTING

12 FRESH BASIL LEAVES

2 OUNCES PROSCIUTTO (APPROXIMATELY 4 SLICES)

1. Preheat the oven to 350°F.
2. Slice the dates lengthwise with a sharp knife, being sure not to cut all of the way through.
3. Spoon a 1 teaspoon of the nut butter inside each date.
4. Sprinkle each date with a light dusting of cayenne, and top with a fresh basil leaf.
5. Slice the prosciutto into 1-inch-long strips. Wrap a slice of prosciutto around each date, and insert a toothpick to secure.
6. Place the prosciutto-wrapped dates on a baking sheet.
7. Bake for 4 to 5 minutes, or until the prosciutto is warm and slightly crispy.

GLUTEN-FREE + DAIRY-FREE + REFINED SUGAR-FREE + PALEO

Frozen Chocolate-Dipped Banana Bites

Makes 16 to 18 bites

Frozen bananas have long been one of our favorite healthy snacks, and these chocolate-dipped, nut butter–stuffed bites take them to the next level. We're talking about a sandwich of nut butter between slices of frozen banana, dipped in rich, velvety dark chocolate, y'all. It's a treat that takes minutes to prepare, and you will be so grateful you did when that sweet tooth hits and all you need to do is reach into your freezer for one of these babies.

⅓ CUP NUT BUTTER OF CHOICE (WE LOVE IT WITH OUR ESPRESSO STOUT NUT BUTTER, PAGE 50)

2 MEDIUM BANANAS, SLICED ¼ INCH THICK

¼ CUP COCONUT OIL

2½ TABLESPOONS UNSWEETENED COCOA POWDER

2 TEASPOONS HONEY OR MAPLE SYRUP

1. Line a baking sheet with parchment paper.
2. Make a sandwich by placing ½ teaspoon of the nut butter between two banana slices. Place on the baking sheet, and repeat the process until the all the banana slices have been used.
3. Transfer the baking sheet to the freezer. Freeze for at least 1 hour, or until the banana slices have hardened.
4. In a small saucepan over medium heat, melt the coconut oil. Whisk in the cocoa powder and honey until well-combined. Remove from the heat, but keep the mixture warm. (You could also microwave the coconut oil, cocoa powder, and maple syrup on high for 15 seconds and stir together.) Please note that the sauce will be quite thin.

Variation + THIS IS A GREAT SNACK ON WHOLE30 IF YOU OPT TO SPRINKLE WITH COCOA POWDER INSTEAD OF DIP IN CHOCOLATE AND USE OUR CLASSIC SMOOTH NUT BUTTER INSTEAD.

GLUTEN-FREE + DAIRY-FREE + VEGAN OPTION + REFINED SUGAR-FREE + PALEO + WHOLE30 OPTION

5. Use tongs to gently dip the banana sandwiches into the chocolate sauce, carefully rolling each one in the sauce until fully coated. Place the chocolate-dipped banana on the baking sheet.

6. At the end, if sauce remains, use a spoon to pour additional chocolate over the bites to fully coat. (Don't fret if your pan is covered in chocolate: It will harden when it freezes, and you'll get some bonus chocolate bites!)

7. Transfer the baking sheet back to the freezer until the chocolate solidifies. Store the bites in an airtight container in the freezer for up to 1 month.

Pro Tip + **ADD FIVE OF THESE BITES TO A BLENDER ALONG WITH 1 CUP OF ALMOND MILK AND 1 CUP OF KALE FOR A SIMPLE AND TASTY SMOOTHIE.**

Clockwise from top: Walnut–Miso Dressing, Honey–Mint Dressing, Creamy Vegan "Alfredo" Sauce

CHAPTER SIX:

Dressings + Sauces

The majority of people we connect with are surprised to learn that nut butters are a natural way to lend flavor and texture to dressings, sauces, marinades, and more. We've loved tinkering around with flavors in the kitchen, creating savory (and sweet!) ways to get saucy with some of our favorite nut butters. The sauces contained in this chapter will be used in other recipes throughout the cookbook, but we encourage you to get creative by finding different uses for them, as well!

Walnut-Miso Dressing

Makes 3/4 cup

We LOVE miso! This Japanese condiment is made from soybeans and adds a unique saltiness and warmth to any dish. If you've ever enjoyed miso soup at your favorite sushi restaurant, it's that kind of soul-warming comfort that we're talking about.

Since miso is a probiotic-rich fermented paste, incorporating it into your diet is also good for your gut. We always like to have it on hand; it's delicious swirled into chicken broth for a quick miso soup or as a salty complement to sauces and dressings, like this one. Paired with nut butter and sweet maple syrup, this sauce is heavenly and also very versatile. Drizzle it on roasted vegetables, or serve it atop our Quinoa Bowls (page 128). We recommend making a batch on Sunday to add to meals throughout the week. This dressing also is delicious with our Ground Up Oregon Hazelnut Butter (page 56) or Cardamom Almond-Cashew Butter (page 47).

⅓ CUP WALNUT-CASHEW BUTTER (PAGE 49)

1½ TABLESPOONS RED MISO PASTE

JUICE FROM ½ LEMON (APPROXIMATELY 1½ TABLESPOONS)

2 TEASPOONS MAPLE SYRUP

¼ TEASPOON MILD CHILI POWDER

⅓ CUP WATER

1. In a small blender, combine the nut butter, miso paste, lemon juice, maple syrup, chili powder, and the water until smooth. (To mix by hand, use ⅓ cup of boiling water instead. Slowly whisk the miso paste and nut butter with the hot water until smooth, then whisk in the remaining ingredients.)
2. Transfer the dressing to an 8-ounce glass jar. It will keep in the refrigerator for up to 1 week.

GLUTEN-FREE + DAIRY-FREE + VEGAN + REFINED SUGAR-FREE

Creamy Pumpkin Seed Dressing

Makes 1½ cups

This rich and creamy pumpkin seed dressing is bright, zesty, and subtly sweet. We love it in hearty salads, such as our Shaved Kale + Pumpkin Seed Salad (page 122), but it also works well as a dip for collard wraps or atop grain bowls.

1 CLOVE GARLIC, MINCED

JUICE OF 1 LEMON (APPROXIMATELY 3 TABLESPOONS)

5 TABLESPOONS EXTRA-VIRGIN OLIVE OIL

¼ CUP PUMPKIN SEED–ALMOND BUTTER (PAGE 52)

1 TABLESPOON MAPLE SYRUP

1 TEASPOON SEA SALT

1. In a small bowl, combine the garlic, lemon juice, olive oil, nut butter, maple syrup, and sea salt. Whisk mixture vigorously until combined, approximately 1 to 2 minutes.
2. The dressing will be quite thick; for a runnier consistency, add ¼ cup of water.
3. Transfer dressing to two (8-ounce) glass jars. It will keep in the refrigerator for up to 1 week.

GLUTEN-FREE + DAIRY-FREE + VEGAN OPTION + REFINED SUGAR-FREE + PALEO

Honey–Mint Dressing

Makes 1 cup

This bright sauce is full of complex and complementary flavors. We love it atop our Sweet Citrus Salad (page 170), but it is also delicious drizzled on avocado toast or a bowl of fresh berries.

¼ CUP CLASSIC SMOOTH NUT BUTTER (PAGE 62)

½ CUP TIGHTLY PACKED FRESH MINT (APPROXIMATELY 3 TO 4 SPRIGS)

2 TABLESPOONS EXTRA-VIRGIN OLIVE OIL

2 TABLESPOONS HONEY

½ TEASPOON SEA SALT

½ TEASPOON APPLE CIDER VINEGAR

¼ CUP WATER

1. In a small blender, combine the nut butter, mint, olive oil, honey, sea salt, vinegar, and water. Process until smooth, 1 to 2 minutes. (For a thinner dressing, add more water until it reaches desired consistency.)
2. Transfer the dressing to an 8-ounce glass jar. It will keep in the refrigerator for up to 3 days.

GLUTEN-FREE + DAIRY-FREE + REFINED SUGAR–FREE + PALEO

Walnut Pesto Sauce

Makes 2/3 cup

Sometimes you just want a quick and herbaceous flavor boost to enhance a simple dish. Look no further than this walnut pesto sauce. It's an easy topping for any roasted vegetable dish, such as our Roasted Carrots (page 136), or served with a crusty baguette and cheese as part of a charcuterie plate.

The recipe below uses a mini blender for the sauce, but if you prefer a chunkier pesto, finely chop the basil instead and mix it together by hand in a bowl with the other ingredients.

1½ CUPS TIGHTLY PACKED BASIL LEAVES, MINCED

½ CUP WALNUT-CASHEW BUTTER (PAGE 49)

JUICE OF 1 LEMON (APPROXIMATELY 3 TABLESPOONS)

½ TEASPOON CRUSHED RED PEPPER

4 TABLESPOONS EXTRA-VIRGIN OLIVE OIL

1. In a medium bowl, combine the basil with the Walnut-Cashew Butter, lemon juice, crushed red pepper, and olive oil. Whisk the pesto vigorously until the ingredients are thoroughly incorporated. (Alternatively, you can also mix this in a small blender.)
2. For a thinner sauce, add water until it reaches the desired consistency.
3. Transfer the mixture to an 8-ounce glass jar. Pesto can be made up to 3 days ahead and stored in the refrigerator.

GLUTEN-FREE + DAIRY-FREE + VEGAN + REFINED SUGAR-FREE + WHOLE30 + PALEO + KETO

Creamy Vegan "Alfredo" Sauce

Makes 2 cups

When we stopped eating dairy, there were certain things we simply accepted we wouldn't be able to enjoy anymore: pizza; sharp cheeses; and certainly creamy, cheesy pasta dishes. So this sauce has been revolutionary for us, not only because it's super simple to make but also because it tastes so decadent and creamy. The nutritional yeast (page 177) lends a "cheesy" taste while the nut butter and chickpeas add depth and texture. Whenever we've made this for friends, the reactions have been consistent—no one can believe there is no cheese or dairy involved!

¼ CUP CLASSIC SMOOTH NUT BUTTER (PAGE 62)

1 (15.5-OUNCE) CAN OF GARBANZO BEANS, DRAINED (OR 1½ CUPS COOKED CHICKPEAS)

2 CLOVES GARLIC, PEELED

¼ CUP EXTRA-VIRGIN OLIVE OIL

1 FRESH SMALL JALAPEÑO, ROUGHLY CHOPPED (OPTIONAL)

JUICE FROM 1½ LEMONS (APPROXIMATELY 4½ TABLESPOONS)

1½ TEASPOONS SEA SALT

6 TABLESPOONS NUTRITIONAL YEAST (PAGE 177)

¼ CUP ALMOND MILK

1. In a blender or food processor fitted with a metal S-shaped blade, combine the nut butter, garbanzo beans, garlic, olive oil, jalapeño, lemon juice, sea salt, and yeast, and pulse until smooth. (Add water, if needed, to thin it out to the desired consistency, starting with ⅛ cup.)
2. Transfer the mixture to a small saucepan over low heat and heat until warm.
3. Any leftover sauce will keep in the refrigerator for up to 5 days.

Note + IF YOU WANT THIS TO MIMIC A TRADITIONAL ALFREDO SAUCE, REMOVE THE JALAPEÑO. BUT TRUST US—IT'S DELICIOUS WITH THE ADDED SPICE. WE ENJOY IT ATOP OUR CHICKPEA PASTA IN OUR CREAMY FENNEL "ALFREDO" (PAGE 134).

GLUTEN-FREE + DAIRY-FREE + VEGAN + REFINED SUGAR-FREE

Cardamom Satay Sauce

Makes 1 cup

Satay sauce is one of our favorite savory ways to use nut butters. Instead of the traditional peanut satay sauce, we like to make them with our almond and hazelnut butters. This cardamom version is a deliciously earthy and rich dipping sauce for everything from chicken skewers to Fresh Spring Rolls (page 140) and our Gado Gado Bowl (page 126). It also serves as a creamy dressing for our Almond Butter Udon Noodles (page 131).

½ CUP CARDAMOM ALMOND-CASHEW BUTTER (PAGE 47)

½ CUP UNSWEETENED COCONUT MILK (LIGHT OR FULL-FAT)

1 TABLESPOON FISH SAUCE

1 TABLESPOON SRIRACHA OR CHILI GARLIC SAUCE (IF AVOIDING SUGAR, USE 1 TEASPOON CRUSHED RED PEPPER FLAKES)

3 TABLESPOONS SESAME OIL

3 TABLESPOONS SOY SAUCE OR COCONUT AMINOS (PAGE 172)

JUICE OF 1 LIME (APPROXIMATELY 2 TABLESPOONS LIME JUICE)

2 CLOVES ROASTED GARLIC (RAW ALSO WORKS)*

2 TABLESPOONS FRESH GINGER, PEELED AND GRATED

1. In a blender or food processor fitted with an S-shaped metal blade, combine the nut butter, coconut milk, fish sauce, sriracha, sesame oil, soy sauce, lime juice, garlic, and ginger. Pulse until smooth. (To mix by hand, mince the garlic beforehand and then whisk in a small bowl.)
2. The sauce will keep in the refrigerator for up to 1 week.

To Roast the Garlic † PREHEAT THE OVEN TO 400°F. WRAP THE CLOVES (OR THE ENTIRE BULB) WITH THE PEEL STILL ON IN ALUMINUM FOIL AND ROAST FOR 30 MINUTES, OR ROAST ON A BAKING SHEET. WE DO THIS AHEAD OF TIME AND ALWAYS TRY TO HAVE SOME ON HAND, AS IT ADDS A DEPTH AND EARTHINESS TO MOST DISHES. STORE THE ROASTED GARLIC IN THE REFRIGERATOR IN A GLASS JAR.

GLUTEN-FREE + DAIRY-FREE + REFINED SUGAR-FREE + PALEO OPTION

Almond Mole Sauce

Makes 4 cups

Our close friends who own a Mexican restaurant in Portland are the ones who initially suggested we include a mole recipe in this cookbook. When they tried the recipe we came up with, they told us that it was the best mole they had ever tasted.

Traditional mole sauces can be quite complex, with over twenty ingredients and hours of cooking time. This recipe is much simpler, using almond butter instead of toasted and pureed nuts. The result is a complex-tasting sauce that hits notes of sweet, bitter, spicy, and savory. It's delicious with chicken, enchiladas, and tacos, such as in our Squash + Cauliflower Tacos (page 132).

2 DRIED ANCHO CHILES

2 TABLESPOONS COCONUT OIL

1 MEDIUM RED ONION, COARSELY CHOPPED

2 CLOVES GARLIC, PEELED AND COARSELY CHOPPED

1 MEDIUM JALAPEÑO, SLICED AND SEEDS REMOVED

½ TEASPOON GROUND CUMIN

½ TEASPOON GROUND OREGANO

½ TEASPOON GROUND CINNAMON

¼ TEASPOON GROUND CLOVE

¼ CUP RAISINS

2 TABLESPOONS TOMATO PASTE

1 CUP CHICKEN OR VEGETABLE BROTH, DIVIDED

¼ CUP ALMOND BUTTER (PAGE 44)

2 TABLESPOONS UNSWEETENED COCOA POWDER

2 TABLESPOONS COCONUT SUGAR

½ TEASPOON SEA SALT

GLUTEN-FREE + DAIRY-FREE + VEGAN + REFINED SUGAR-FREE + PALEO

1. Place the dried ancho chiles in a bowl of hot water for at least 30 minutes to soften.
2. Heat the coconut oil in a skillet over medium-high heat. Add the onion, garlic, and jalapeño, and sauté about 5 minutes or until the onion is translucent.
3. Add the cumin, oregano, cinnamon, and clove, and continue to cook for an additional 3 to 4 minutes.
4. Decrease the heat to medium; stir in the raisins and tomato paste. Cook an additional 1 to 2 minutes.
5. Add in ½ cup of the broth; cook an additional 4 to 5 minutes, stirring up any bits that are sticking to the bottom of the pan.
6. When the mixture has reduced by half and the onions are fully cooked, remove from the heat. Allow to cool slightly, then transfer the mixture to a food processor fitted with an S-shaped metal blade or a heavy-duty blender.
7. Remove the ancho chiles from the water, drain them, and remove the stems.
8. Add the ancho chiles, almond butter, cocoa powder, coconut sugar, sea salt, and the remaining ½ cup of broth.
9. Process the mixture for 4 to 5 minutes, until the sauce is smooth and fully blended.
10. Transfer the cooled mole into an airtight container. The sauce will keep in the refrigerator for up to 3 days or in the freezer for up to 6 months.

Note † WHILE THIS SAUCE IS QUITE THICK AND CHUNKY, YOU COULD ADD MORE WATER OR BROTH TO THIN IT OUT IF YOU PREFER.

Almond Butter–Ginger Marinade

Makes 1/4 cup

This Indonesian-inspired marinade is rich, nutty, and full of flavor. We recommend using it to marinate vegetables, tempeh, tofu, or chicken, such as in our Marinated Chicken Skewers (page 121).

1 TABLESPOON ALMOND BUTTER (PAGE 44)

1 TABLESPOON SESAME OIL

2 CLOVES GARLIC

1 TABLESPOON SOY SAUCE OR COCONUT AMINOS (PAGE 172)

¼ TEASPOON CRUSHED RED PEPPER FLAKES (OR SUBSTITUTE ½ TABLESPOON SRIRACHA OR CHILI GARLIC SAUCE)

1 TEASPOON GROUND CUMIN

½ TEASPOON GROUND GINGER

½ TEASPOON SEA SALT

1. In a small bowl, whisk together the nut butter, sesame oil, garlic, soy sauce, red pepper flakes, cumin, ginger, and sea salt.
2. If not using right away, transfer the marinade to a 4-ounce glass jar to store. It will keep refrigerated for up to 3 days.

GLUTEN-FREE + DAIRY-FREE + VEGAN + REFINED SUGAR-FREE + WHOLE30 + PALEO + KETO

CHAPTER SEVEN:

Savory

Adding a nut butter to even a simple recipe can be such an easy and quick way to add a punch of flavor or texture to a dish. We'll show you that nut butter doesn't always have to always be paired with fruit and chocolate (although, obviously, we love that, too). Think toasted walnuts with red pepper, the crunch of hazelnuts in a warm bacon salad, or pumpkin seed dressing providing a creamy coating for bitter brassicas. There is a whole world we are excited for you to discover!

Muhammara (Walnut Red Pepper Dip)

Makes 2 cups

Move over, hummus. Muhammara is the new Middle Eastern dip that we can't get enough of. Composed primarily of red peppers and walnuts, this hearty dip is nutty, subtly sweet, and just a tad spicy. It's traditionally made with pomegranate molasses, freshly charred Aleppo peppers, and breadcrumbs. Here, we not only lighten it up by replacing breadcrumbs with almond flour but also we make it easier by simplifying the ingredient list and overall effort involved. (You're welcome!) This is *always* a hit at parties—we love serving it alongside rice crackers and crudités as an appetizer.

1 (12-OUNCE) JAR OF ROASTED RED PEPPERS

6 TABLESPOONS WALNUT-CASHEW BUTTER (PAGE 49)

½ TABLESPOON EXTRA-VIRGIN OLIVE OIL

½ TABLESPOON MAPLE SYRUP (OPTIONAL)

½ CLOVE GARLIC, PEELED

JUICE OF ⅓ LEMON (APPROXIMATELY 1 TABLESPOON)

½ CUP ALMOND FLOUR

PINCH OF RED PEPPER FLAKES

¼ TEASPOON CUMIN

¼ TEASPOON OREGANO

⅛ TEASPOON SEA SALT

3 TABLESPOONS WALNUTS, TOASTED, FOR GARNISH

FRESH PARSLEY, CHOPPED, FOR GARNISH

GLUTEN-FREE + DAIRY-FREE + VEGAN + REFINED SUGAR-FREE + PALEO OPTION + KETO OPTION

1. Drain the liquid from the jar of roasted red peppers, and pat the peppers dry with a paper towel to remove excess moisture.
2. In a food processor fitted with an S-shaped metal blade, combine the red peppers, nut butter, olive oil, maple syrup, garlic, lemon juice, almond flour, red pepper flakes, cumin, oregano, and sea salt. Process for 1 to 2 minutes, until fully incorporated.
3. Add the toasted walnuts and pulse quickly for an additional 10 to 15 seconds. (Adding these at the end maintains a nice, chunky texture to the dip—and enhances the walnut flavor.)
4. Transfer the dip to a bowl, and garnish with the fresh parsley.
5. Serve at room temperature with crackers or crudités. It will keep in the refrigerator for up to 1 week, so we suggest making it ahead of time.

Badrijani (Eggplant–Walnut Rolls)

Makes 15 to 18 rolls

Badrijani is a Georgian (think the country, not the state) dish consisting of fried eggplant rolls in a savory walnut paste. It's traditionally made with raw walnuts, but using toasted walnut butter makes it easier to put together—and more flavorful. It can be enjoyed on its own as an appetizer, alongside crostini, or atop a light frisée salad. Prepare the filling ahead of time so that the flavors have time to meld. Since these are best served cold or at room temperature, they also make a great picnic snack!

⅔ CUP WALNUT–CASHEW BUTTER (PAGE 49)

2 CLOVES OF GARLIC, PEELED AND MINCED

1 TEASPOON WHITE WINE VINEGAR

2½ TEASPOONS GROUND CORIANDER

¾ TEASPOON GROUND FENUGREEK

PINCH OF CHILI POWDER

⅓ CUP WATER

3 MEDIUM CHINESE EGGPLANTS

SEA SALT

¼ CUP CANOLA OIL OR COCONUT OIL, FOR FRYING

FLAKY SEA SALT, FOR GARNISH

FRESH PARSLEY, CHOPPED, FOR GARNISH

POMEGRANATE SEEDS, FOR GARNISH

GLUTEN-FREE + DAIRY-FREE + VEGAN + REFINED SUGAR-FREE + WHOLE30 + PALEO + KETO

1. In a mixing bowl (or in a small blender), combine the nut butter, garlic, white wine vinegar, coriander, fenugreek, chili powder, and water until incorporated.
2. Transfer the paste to the refrigerator to store for at least 1 hour before using. It may be made up to 2 days in advance.
3. Cut the tops off the eggplants. Slice them lengthwise into long, thin slices, approximately ½-inch thick.
4. Lay the slices out on a baking sheet and salt generously. Let them stand for 30 minutes, then pat dry with a paper towel. (This removes bitterness.)
5. Line a separate baking sheet with paper towels.
6. Heat 2 to 3 tablespoons of oil in a large skillet over medium-high heat. Add a few eggplant slices (arrange in a single layer, as many as you can fit in the pan) and cook for 4 to 6 minutes per side. Once the eggplant has browned on both sides and is floppy but not yet crisp, transfer to the paper towel–lined baking sheet.
7. Continue until all slices are fried, adding more oil if the pan gets dry.
8. Scoop approximately 1 tablespoon of paste onto each eggplant slice, and spread to cover the slice. Roll it up lengthwise (using a toothpick to secure, if necessary) and transfer to a plate.
9. Top each eggplant roll with a sprinkle of flaky sea salt, fresh parsley, and pomegranate seeds.
10. Serve at room temperature with crackers or crostini or with a light frisée salad. These can also be made up to 3 days ahead of time and kept in an airtight container in the refrigerator.

Warm Hazelnut-Bacon Salad

Serves 2

Is there any salad more decadent than one coated in a warm bacon dressing? The beauty of this salad lies in its simplicity, and, of course, in the bacon fat. (You really can't go wrong when you cook vegetables in bacon fat.) With only one skillet and 30 minutes' time, you can create a comforting yet complex salad. While we don't do dairy, we've been told that this is delicious with blue cheese crumbles, as well!

4 SLICES BACON

1 SMALL ZUCCHINI, THINLY SLICED

½ LARGE WHITE ONION, THINLY SLICED

1 TABLESPOON APPLE CIDER VINEGAR

3 TABLESPOONS OREGON HAZELNUT BUTTER (PAGE 56)

1 TABLESPOON OLIVE OIL

¼ HEAD RED CABBAGE, THINLY SLICED

6 CUPS LOOSELY PACKED SPINACH

2 TABLESPOONS CHOPPED TOASTED HAZELNUTS

2 LEMON WEDGES

1. Lay the bacon strips on a cold skillet. Heat to medium-high, and cook the bacon 4 to 6 minutes, or until crispy. Drain and reserve the bacon fat, leaving a thin coating in the skillet and reserving the rest in a small jar or bowl. Transfer the strips to a plate; keep warm.
2. Add the zucchini and onion to the skillet. Sauté them in the bacon fat for 5 to 7 minutes, or until the onions are soft and translucent. Transfer to a plate; keep warm.
3. If the skillet does not have any bacon fat left coating the bottom, add the extra back to the skillet (1 to 2 tablespoons). Decrease the heat to low. Add the apple cider vinegar and bring to a boil, scraping up the browned bits with a metal spatula. Add the nut butter and olive oil, whisking to incorporate. Remove from the heat.

(CONTINUED)

GLUTEN-FREE + DAIRY-FREE + REFINED SUGAR-FREE + PALEO

4. Place the sliced cabbage and spinach leaves in the warm skillet, and toss to quickly coat in the hazelnut–bacon dressing.
5. Crumble the bacon strips.
6. Divide the dressed salad between two bowls, then top each with the bacon crumbles, zucchini, onion, and toasted hazelnuts. Serve warm and enjoy immediately, with lemon wedges.

Marinated Chicken Skewers

Serves 4, as an appetizer

Chicken? Nut butter? Yes, please. Marinated in our Almond Butter–Ginger Marinade, these skewers are just as delicious grilled as they are baked. If you want to go all in on the almond butter theme, serve them alongside our Cardamom Satay Sauce (page 109). You will need eight to ten wooden skewers to make these.

1 POUND BONELESS, SKINLESS CHICKEN TENDERS

¼ CUP ALMOND BUTTER–GINGER MARINADE (PAGE 112)

FRESH CILANTRO, CHOPPED, FOR GARNISH

4 LIME WEDGES, FOR GARNISH

1. In a medium-size bowl, combine the chicken tenders with the marinade, and toss to coat.
2. Cover the strips with plastic wrap, and transfer to the refrigerator to marinate for at least 1 hour, but preferably overnight.
3. When ready to cook, preheat the oven to 400°F.
4. Line a large baking sheet with aluminum foil. Thread a piece of chicken through the wooden skewer, and place on the baking sheet. Repeat until all chicken has been skewered.
5. Bake for 12 to 15 minutes, or until the chicken reaches 165°F degrees on a meat thermometer and the juices run clear.
6. Transfer skewers to a serving platter and serve with the cilantro and lime wedges.

GLUTEN-FREE + DAIRY-FREE + REFINED SUGAR-FREE + WHOLE30 + PALEO + KETO

Shaved Kale + Pumpkin Seed Salad

Serves 4

We love a good kale salad, and this is our current favorite. The brassicas become tender and sweet when massaged and coated in this creamy dressing, which is topped with toasted pumpkin seeds and currants to complete the autumnal vibe. If you want to make it heartier, add roasted delicata squash or crumbled feta. This salad is great to make a day or two ahead of time and keep refrigerated; it holds up well. Save yourself time and chopping by using the food processor's shredding attachment to shred the vegetables.

4 CUPS FINELY SHREDDED LACINATO KALE (APPROXIMATELY 1 BUNCH)

2 CUPS FINELY SHREDDED CABBAGE (APPROXIMATELY ¼ HEAD)

2 CUPS FINELY SHREDDED BRUSSELS SPROUTS (10 TO 15 SPROUTS)

JUICE OF ½ LEMON (APPROXIMATELY 1½ TABLESPOONS)

PINCH OF SEA SALT

1 CUP CREAMY PUMPKIN SEED DRESSING (PAGE 105)

2 TABLESPOONS DRIED CURRANTS

2 TABLESPOONS PUMPKIN SEEDS, TOASTED

1. Place the kale, cabbage, and brussels sprouts in a large salad bowl. Add the lemon juice and sea salt, and massage by hand into the vegetables until tender. Let stand for 10 to 15 minutes to soften.
2. Toss the salad with the dressing.
3. Transfer the salad to a serving bowl, and garnish with the currants and toasted pumpkin seeds.
4. The salad can be made ahead and stored in the refrigerator for up to 3 days.

GLUTEN-FREE + DAIRY-FREE + VEGAN OPTION + REFINED SUGAR-FREE + PALEO

Almond Butter Miso Soup

Serves 2 to 3

On a cold winter evening, there is nothing better than curling up with a bowl of noodle soup. This one incorporates two of our favorite things—miso and almond butter—for a luxuriously rich and creamy broth. The almond butter adds a nuttiness, balancing out the tangy miso. With notes of fresh ginger, garlic, and sesame, this soup is great if you feel like you're fighting a cold and need an immune boost. This recipe makes two heaping bowls of noodle soup or three modest-size portions.

2 TABLESPOONS SESAME OIL

½ MEDIUM WHITE ONION, FINELY DICED

5 WHITE MUSHROOMS, THINLY SLICED

2 CLOVES OF GARLIC, MINCED

1 TABLESPOON FRESHLY GRATED GINGER

4 CUPS WATER

2-INCH PIECE OF KOMBU (OPTIONAL)

4 TABLESPOONS RED MISO PASTE

2 TABLESPOONS CLASSIC SMOOTH NUT BUTTER (PAGE 62)

4 OUNCES RICE NOODLES

1 CUP LOOSELY PACKED SPINACH

FRESH CILANTRO, CHOPPED, FOR GARNISH

2 LIME WEDGES, FOR GARNISH

RED PEPPER FLAKES, FOR GARNISH

GLUTEN-FREE + DAIRY-FREE + VEGAN + REFINED SUGAR-FREE

1. In a medium-size saucepan, heat the sesame oil over medium-high heat.
2. Add the onion, mushrooms, garlic, and ginger. Simmer, covered, until tender and fragrant, approximately 8 to 10 minutes. Stir occasionally to avoid sticking.
3. Add the water to the saucepan and increase heat to bring to a boil. Add in the kombu if using.
4. Once the water is boiling, reduce heat to a simmer. Stir in the miso paste and nut butter, whisking gently until dissolved.
5. Add the rice noodles and spinach. Cook for an additional 8 to 10 minutes, stirring occasionally, until the noodles are fully cooked.
6. Remove the kombu if using. Divide the soup between two or three bowls.
7. Top with the cilantro and serve with a wedge of lime. Sprinkle with the red pepper flakes.

Gado Gado Bowl

Serves 4

A little-known fact about Carolyn: She spent a few months living in Bali helping to run a vegan coconut ice cream company. During her time there, she was introduced to gado gado, an Indonesian dish that is a vegetarian's dream. You can find it on most street corners and restaurants in Bali. It's traditionally composed of fried rice, potatoes, cabbage, tomatoes, green beans, crispy tempeh, and prawn chips surrounding a *bowl* of delicious peanut satay sauce. You can eat it as a dip with the veggies in the sauce or mix it all together for a sort of salad. We love its versatility and also how well it works as a make-ahead meal during our Sunday meal prep. This is also delicious served with Marinated Chicken Skewers (page 121) or with panfried tempeh.

2 SMALL SWEET POTATOES, SLICED INTO ¼-INCH SLICES

1 TABLESPOON EXTRA-VIRGIN OLIVE OIL

1¼ TEASPOON SEA SALT, DIVIDED

1 CUP GREEN BEANS (APPROXIMATELY 40 BEANS)

1 CUP CARDAMOM SATAY SAUCE (PAGE 109)

¾ CUP SHORT-GRAIN COOKED BROWN RICE

4 HARD-BOILED EGGS, SLICED

¼ HEAD GREEN OR PURPLE CABBAGE, THINLY SLICED

2 RIPE TOMATOES OR RED BELL PEPPERS, SLICED

ROUGHLY CHOPPED FRESH CILANTRO, FOR GARNISH

2 HANDFULS OF BEAN SPROUTS

GLUTEN-FREE + DAIRY-FREE + REFINED SUGAR-FREE

3. Bring 2 quarts of water and the remaining 1 teaspoon of sea salt to a boil in a large saucepan over high heat. Add the green beans and cook until tender-crisp, about 3 minutes. Drain, rinse with ice-cold water, and drain again.

4. Assemble the plates: Divide the sauce between four small bowls. Place each bowl in the center of a plate. In a circle surrounding the plate, add the cooked rice, sliced eggs, sweet potatoes, green beans, cabbage, tomatoes, cilantro, and bean sprouts. (If serving for a crowd, you could also arrange all of the vegetables on one large tray with the sauce in the middle. Let guests assemble their own small plates.)

1. Preheat the oven to 400°F.

2. Place the sweet potato slices on a baking sheet. Coat with the olive oil and sprinkle with ¼ teaspoon of the sea salt. Bake for 15 to 20 minutes, until the sweet potatoes are soft when pierced with a fork.

Broccoli Quinoa Bowls with Walnut-Miso Dressing

Makes 4 servings

Don't be deceived by this recipe's simplicity; this quinoa bowl is seriously delicious. The walnut-miso dressing elevates a meal that may otherwise seem average and takes it to a new and more interesting level. It has become a staple in our weekly Sunday meal prep since it's easy to make the elements ahead of time and assemble throughout the week. We include sweet potato and broccoli, but you could swap any vegetable, bean, or meat.

¼ HEAD PURPLE CABBAGE, THINLY SLICED

3 TABLESPOONS APPLE CIDER VINEGAR

1¼ TEASPOON SEA SALT, DIVIDED

1 LARGE HEAD OF BROCCOLI, ROUGHLY CHOPPED

1 LARGE SWEET POTATO, PEELED AND CUT INTO ½-INCH CUBES

2 TABLESPOONS COCONUT OIL, MELTED

1 TEASPOON DRIED OREGANO

½ TEASPOON BLACK PEPPER

3 CUPS WATER

1½ CUPS QUINOA

¾ CUP WALNUT-MISO DRESSING (PAGE 104)

1 RIPE AVOCADO, SLICED

⅓ CUP CHOPPED TOASTED WALNUTS, FOR GARNISH

HANDFUL OF CHOPPED CILANTRO, FOR GARNISH

GLUTEN-FREE + DAIRY-FREE + VEGAN + REFINED SUGAR-FREE

1. Preheat the oven to 400°F. Line a baking sheet with parchment paper.
2. In a bowl, combine the cabbage with the vinegar and ½ teaspoon of the sea salt. Massage by hand for 1 minute, then set aside for at least 15 minutes, allowing it to quickly pickle. It's done when the cabbage is tender and some juice is in the bottom of the bowl.
3. Place the broccoli and sweet potato in an even layer on the baking sheet, and season with the coconut oil, ½ teaspoon of the sea salt, the dried oregano, and black pepper.
4. Transfer the pan to the oven and bake for 20 to 25 minutes, until the sweet potato is soft when pierced with a fork and the broccoli is lightly charred.
5. Meanwhile, in a medium saucepan, combine the water with the quinoa and the remaining ¼ teaspoon of sea salt. Bring to a boil, cover, and reduce to simmer for 15 minutes. Remove from the heat, let sit for 5 minutes, and then fluff with a fork.

6. Divide the quinoa mixture between four bowls. Top each with ¼ serving of the sweet potato, broccoli, and cabbage. Drizzle 3 tablespoons of the dressing over each. Garnish with the sliced avocado, chopped walnuts, and cilantro.

Almond Butter Udon Noodles

Serves 6

Ready for a cozy night in? A twist on your classic Thai peanut noodle recipe, this udon noodle dish shares the same nutty, comforting qualities but is brightened by the almond and cardamom flavors. It's traditionally served cold, making it a great make-ahead dish for potlucks or Sunday meal prep.

1 (10-OUNCE) PACKAGE UDON NOODLES (FOR GLUTEN-FREE, USE RICE NOODLES OR SOBA NOODLES)

4 CUPS SHREDDED CABBAGE (APPROXIMATELY ¼ HEAD)

2 CUPS SHREDDED CARROT (1 TO 2 CARROTS)

1 CUP CARDAMOM SATAY SAUCE (PAGE 109)

SEA SALT, FOR SEASONING (OPTIONAL)

5 SCALLIONS, COARSELY CHOPPED

¼ CUP CHOPPED TOASTED CASHEWS

HANDFUL OF FRESH CILANTRO, COARSELY CHOPPED

2 LIMES, SLICED INTO WEDGES

1. Bring 6 quarts of water to a boil. Add the noodles, and cook according to package instructions. Drain and run under cold water.
2. Combine the cabbage and shredded carrot in a large bowl with the noodles.
3. Add the satay sauce and mix until thoroughly incorporated. (If desired, add more sea salt to taste.)
4. Garnish with the scallions, cashews, and cilantro.
5. Serve with lime wedges. This can be made up to 2 days ahead of time and stored in the refrigerator.

GLUTEN-FREE OPTION + DAIRY-FREE + REFINED SUGAR-FREE

Squash + Cauliflower Tacos with Almond Mole

Makes 12 tacos

We all know tacos are always a hit if you're feeding a crowd. Who doesn't love a flavorful DIY meal?! The corn tortillas are gluten-free, but if you're following a grain-free diet, you could also assemble these as a salad by layering the mole, squash, and cauliflower atop a bed of greens. The mole sauce is uniquely rich and complex, so we keep this recipe simple to really let it shine.

2 CUPS SHREDDED CABBAGE

3 TABLESPOONS APPLE CIDER VINEGAR

1¼ TEASPOON SEA SALT, DIVIDED

1 MEDIUM BUTTERNUT SQUASH, PEELED AND DICED

1 HEAD OF CAULIFLOWER, BROKEN INTO FLORETS

3 TABLESPOONS COCONUT OIL, MELTED

2 TABLESPOONS GROUND CUMIN

1 TABLESPOON MILD CHILI POWDER

1 TABLESPOON DRIED OREGANO

12 (6-INCH) CORN TORTILLAS

2 AVOCADOS, SLICED

1 CUP ALMOND MOLE SAUCE (PAGE 110)

SESAME SEEDS, FOR GARNISH

GLUTEN-FREE + DAIRY-FREE + VEGAN + REFINED SUGAR-FREE

1. Preheat the oven to 375°F.
2. In a bowl, combine the cabbage with the apple cider vinegar and ½ teaspoon of the sea salt. Massage by hand for 1 minute, then set aside for at least 15 minutes, allowing it to quickly pickle. It's done when the cabbage is tender and some juice is in the bottom of the bowl.
3. In a large bowl, mix together the squash and cauliflower with the coconut oil, cumin, chili powder, oregano, and the remaining ¾ teaspoon of sea salt until the vegetables are fully coated in oil and spices.
4. Transfer the vegetables to a baking dish, and bake for 40 to 45 minutes, until tender when pierced with a fork but still moist.
5. Wrap the tortillas in foil and warm them in the oven for 2 to 3 minutes.
6. Place 1⁄12 serving of the cauliflower and squash in the center of the warm tortilla. Top with the shredded cabbage and avocado. Roll up the taco and continue with the remaining tortillas until all of the filling is used.
7. In a small saucepan, warm the mole sauce, and pour it on top of the tacos. Sprinkle the tacos with the sesame seeds. Serve warm.

Creamy Fennel "Alfredo"

Serves 4 to 6

This dairy-free, grain-free pasta dish is revolutionary for anyone who yearns for creamy pasta but hates the feeling of being weighed down by all of that gluten and dairy. Decadent and rich but not heavy, the star of this dish is really the fennel. It's complemented by the bright and zesty sauce, which manages to taste "cheesy" but not overpowering. We enjoy it with a bit of crumbled sausage, but that is completely optional. If you prefer it to be more like a traditional Alfredo sauce, omit the jalapeño from the sauce and add in roasted cherry tomatoes.

1 LARGE FENNEL BULB

1 TABLESPOON EXTRA-VIRGIN OLIVE OIL

4 CUPS TIGHTLY PACKED SPINACH

1 (8-OUNCE) BOX CHICKPEA PASTA (WE RECOMMEND BANZA'S ROTINI)

2 CUPS CREAMY VEGAN "ALFREDO" SAUCE (PAGE 108)

10 OUNCES COOKED SAUSAGE, COARSELY CHOPPED (OPTIONAL)

HANDFUL OF CHOPPED FRESH BASIL

1. Prepare the fennel by cutting off the green stalks, leaving only the white bulb. Remove any wilted outer layers. Cut the bulb in half and then thinly slice it in a crosswise direction.
2. Heat the olive oil in a large skillet over medium-high heat. Add the fennel and sauté approximately 6 to 8 minutes, or until translucent. Add the spinach, cover the skillet, and remove from the heat so that the spinach wilts.
3. Cook the pasta according to package directions, approximately 8 to 10 minutes, and drain in a colander.
4. In a saucepan over medium heat, warm the "Alfredo" sauce.

GLUTEN-FREE + DAIRY-FREE + VEGAN + REFINED SUGAR-FREE

5. In a large bowl, combine the pasta and 1 cup of the warm sauce. Stir, and slowly add the remaining 1 cup of sauce until all the pasta is coated. (You may not need the full second cup.)
6. Stir in the fennel, spinach, and sausage if using.
7. Garnish the pasta with the basil and serve warm.

Variation + THIS RECIPE ALSO WORKS WITH REGULAR PASTA, BUT IF YOU HAVEN'T TRIED CHICKPEA PASTA YET . . . GIVE IT A GO! IT TASTES JUST LIKE THE REAL THING, WE PROMISE.

Roasted Carrots with Walnut Pesto Sauce

Serves 4, as a side dish

This is an effortless dish that's perfect for throwing together when you have guests coming over. We served it as a side last Thanksgiving, and it was a massive hit. The best part? It's Whole30-friendly and composed simply of vegetables and healthy fats. It's also delicious with sweet potato wedges.

3 POUNDS CARROTS (APPROXIMATELY 14 TO 16 CARROTS), PEELED AND CUT INTO 3-INCH MATCHSTICKS

2 TABLESPOONS EXTRA-VIRGIN OLIVE OIL, PLUS EXTRA FOR SERVING

1 TEASPOON SEA SALT

½ TEASPOON BLACK PEPPER

⅔ CUP WALNUT PESTO SAUCE (PAGE 107)

CHOPPED FRESH PARSLEY, FOR GARNISH

⅓ CUP WALNUTS, TOASTED, FOR GARNISH

1. Preheat the oven to 400°F.
2. Divide the carrots between two baking sheets. Drizzle each with olive oil, and sprinkle with the sea salt and black pepper. Toss to coat, then arrange the carrots evenly in a single layer.
3. Roast the carrots for 25 to 30 minutes, or until tender. (For crispier carrots, broil them for the last few minutes to get a nice char.)
4. Remove the carrots from the oven and arrange on a large serving platter. Drizzle with the pesto, then top with a drizzle of olive oil, the fresh parsley, and toasted walnuts. Serve warm.

GLUTEN-FREE + DAIRY-FREE + VEGAN + REFINED SUGAR-FREE + WHOLE30 + PALEO + KETO

Hazelnut Butter Chicken Legs

Serves 2

One of our farmers' market regulars first sparked the idea for this recipe. He shared that he loved to coat oven-roasted chicken with our hazelnut butter. He described his process in depth to us—massaging the nut butter into the chicken skin, adding fragrant herbs like rosemary, and finishing it with toasted hazelnuts for an added crunch. Our mouths were watering, and we set out to re-create this dish immediately.

The recipe below is a riff on his, and while we make it with chicken legs, you could also use thighs, wings, or even a whole chicken if you're feeling ambitious. We use fresh rosemary, garlic, and lemon to brighten up this wintry dish. We love making this recipe on a cold night and enjoying it with a glass of red wine; it's just one of those meals that soothes the soul. We hope you cozy up and enjoy this as much as we do.

5 LARGE PARSNIPS, CUT INTO 2-INCH MATCHSTICKS

10 MEDIUM SHALLOTS, CUT INTO QUARTERS

2 TABLESPOONS GHEE OR UNSALTED BUTTER, MELTED

1¼ TEASPOONS SEA SALT, DIVIDED, PLUS EXTRA

2 LEMONS

4 CLOVES OF GARLIC, PEELED, DIVIDED

2 SPRIGS OF FRESH ROSEMARY

2 BONE-IN, SKIN-ON CHICKEN LEGS

2 TABLESPOONS EXTRA-VIRGIN OLIVE OIL

¼ TEASPOON BLACK PEPPER

¼ CUP OREGON HAZELNUT BUTTER (PAGE 56)

½ TEASPOON CHILI POWDER

2 TEASPOONS APPLE CIDER VINEGAR

2 CUPS LOOSELY PACKED FRISÉE OR BUTTER LETTUCE, RINSED AND COARSELY CHOPPED

CHOPPED TOASTED HAZELNUTS, FOR GARNISH

GLUTEN-FREE + DAIRY-FREE + REFINED SUGAR-FREE + PALEO + WHOLE30 OPTION

1. Preheat the oven to 375°F.
2. Place the parsnips and shallots on a baking sheet and toss to coat with the melted ghee and ½ teaspoon of the sea salt.
3. Thinly slice one of the lemons and add half of the slices to the baking sheet, nestling them in with the vegetables. Add three cloves of the garlic and the rosemary to the baking sheet.
4. Place the baking sheet in the oven, and bake for 40 to 45 minutes, or until the parsnips are tender when pierced with a fork and the shallots are soft and translucent.
5. Meanwhile, coat the chicken legs with the olive oil, ½ teaspoon of the sea salt, and the black pepper.
6. Place the chicken legs in a roasting pan and tuck the remaining lemon slices around them. Place the pan in the oven and cook for 25 minutes.
7. Mince the remaining clove of garlic. Combine it in a small bowl with the nut butter, chili powder, the remaining ¼ teaspoon of sea salt, and the apple cider vinegar.
8. Remove the chicken legs after 25 minutes, and coat each in the nut butter mixture.
9. Return to the oven, and bake for an additional 5 to 10 minutes, or until the internal temperature of the chicken reaches 165°F and the juices run clear.
10. In a small bowl, combine ¼ cup of the chicken drippings (the juice remaining at the bottom of the chicken's roasting pan) with the juice of the remaining lemon, plus sea salt to taste.
11. Toss this dressing with the frisée and divide the salad between two plates. Place a chicken leg and ¼ of the roasted vegetables on each plate. Garnish with the hazelnuts.

Fresh Spring Rolls with Cardamom Satay Sauce

Makes 8 Spring Rolls

Always keep rice paper wrappers (and nut butter) on hand. They make the best last-minute dinner, especially on a hot summer night when you can't bear to turn on the stove. Throw any fresh veggies, tofu, or cooked meat you have in the fridge into the papers, whip up a quick dipping sauce, and you're good to go. (It looks pretty impressive for the minimal effort, too!)

Here, we pair these with the Cardamom Satay Sauce (page 109), but they would also be delicious served with the Creamy Pumpkin Seed Dressing (page 105)!

8 (6-INCH) RICE PAPER WRAPS ("SPRING ROLL SKINS")

1 MANGO, SLICED

½ RIPE PITTED AVOCADO, SLICED

½ MEDIUM CUCUMBER, SLICED

8 OUNCES EXTRA-FIRM TOFU, SLICED, OR COOKED SHRIMP, PEELED (FRESH, OR FROZEN AND DEFROSTED)

HANDFUL OF FRESH MINT LEAVES

1 CUP CARDAMOM SATAY SAUCE (PAGE 109)

1. Fill a large, shallow dish with ½ inch of hot tap water. Place one rice paper wrap in the water for 15 to 30 seconds, or until the wrap is soft and pliable.
2. Transfer to a clean work surface, and place one to two slices of the mango, avocado, cucumber, and tofu in the center. Top with a few mint leaves.
3. Fold half the wrapper over the fillings, fold in the top and bottom, then roll up the wrapper securely. Repeat rolling remaining ingredients into remaining wraps.
4. Serve immediately, alongside the sauce.

GLUTEN-FREE + DAIRY-FREE + REFINED SUGAR-FREE OPTION

CHAPTER EIGHT:

Sweet Treats

Congrats! You made it all the way to the end, so we will reward you with what you really came here for—exploring all of the delicious ways to pair nut butters with chocolate (and other sweet treats!). The natural sweetness of many tree nuts can be beautifully highlighted in dessert recipes, and oftentimes they serve as a replacement for dairy and gluten. Here, we'll show you how to make the most decadent grain-free brownies, a mind-blowing cardamom frosting, a simple citrus salad, and more.

Fudgy Walnut Brownies

Makes 16 small brownies

We think these walnut brownies are heavenly, so much so that even we can't believe that they are refined sugar- and gluten-free. You won't believe your taste buds! Chocolaty, rich, and moist, they are swirled with toasted walnuts and chocolate chips, then finished with flaky sea salt. Bake up a batch to share at your next potluck, and you'll be sure to impress.

¾ CUP OF WALNUT-CASHEW BUTTER (PAGE 49), PLUS 2 TABLESPOONS FOR SWIRL

½ CUP COCONUT SUGAR

¾ CUP UNSWEETENED APPLESAUCE

½ CUP UNSWEETENED ALMOND MILK

2 TABLESPOONS MAPLE SYRUP

1 TEASPOON VANILLA EXTRACT, OR SEEDS FROM 1 VANILLA BEAN

1 CUP UNSWEETENED NATURAL COCOA POWDER

⅓ CUP OAT FLOUR

1 TEASPOON BAKING SODA

¾ TEASPOON SEA SALT

1 CUP VEGAN CHOCOLATE CHIPS

1 CUP TOASTED WALNUTS, CHOPPED

FLAKY SEA SALT, FOR FINISHING

1. Preheat the oven to 350°F. Line an 8 by 8-inch pan with parchment paper.
2. Using a hand mixer or wooden spoon, mix together ¾ cup of the nut butter, the coconut sugar, applesauce, almond milk, maple syrup, and vanilla.
3. Add in the cocoa powder, oat flour, baking soda, and salt. Mix until fully incorporated.
4. Fold in the chocolate chips and chopped walnuts.
5. With a spatula, transfer the batter to the parchment-lined pan. Swirl the remaining 2 tablespoons of nut butter on top. (Use a toothpick or knife to etch in a pretty crosshatch pattern for a stunning visual effect.)
6. Bake the brownies for 45 to 50 minutes, or until the top is firm to the touch and begins to crack. Sprinkle with the flaky sea salt.
7. Allow the brownies to cool completely. Transfer to an airtight container to store for up to 5 days.

GLUTEN-FREE | DAIRY FREE + VEGAN

Apple Crisp

Makes 1 (9-inch) crisp

Sweet cinnamon, juicy apples, and toasted oats . . . who can resist the smell of apple crisp baking in the oven? We have made this recipe countless times over the past few years; it's especially great for potlucks or when we're graced with a bounty of fresh fruit. Not only is this crisp easy to whip together but also it is an excellent way to highlight whatever fruit is in season. Apples have a long autumnal season here in Oregon, so we've included a recipe with those—but feel free to use any fruit you have on hand. We've also made it with blueberries and peaches, and the results are superb.

6 CUPS PEELED, THINLY SLICED GALA APPLES (APPROXIMATELY 6 MEDIUM APPLES)

1 TEASPOON SEA SALT, DIVIDED

JUICE OF ½ LEMON (APPROXIMATELY 1½ TABLESPOONS)

1 CUP OLD-FASHIONED ROLLED OATS (SEE NOTE)

¾ CUP CINNAMON SNICKERDOODLE NUT BUTTER (PAGE 54)

½ CUP COCONUT SUGAR

ICE CREAM OF CHOICE, FOR SERVING

1. Preheat the oven to 350°F.
2. Combine the apple slices in a large bowl with ¼ teaspoon of the sea salt and the lemon juice, stirring until the apples are fully coated.
3. Spoon the apples to a 9-inch pie pan.
4. In a large bowl, make the crumble by combining the oats, nut butter, coconut sugar, and the remaining ¾ teaspoon of sea salt. Use your fingers to mix it together until evenly incorporated.
5. Top the apples with the crumble, evenly distributing and pressing firmly down to fill any holes.

GLUTEN-FREE + DAIRY-FREE + VEGAN + REFINED SUGAR-FREE + PALEO

6. Cover the pie pan with foil and bake for 50 to 55 minutes. Bake until the apples are fully cooked and apple juice starts bubbling up around the sides.

7. For a particularly crispy crumble topping, remove the foil and broil the crisp at 500°F for an additional 1 to 2 minutes.

8. Serve warm with the ice cream. Any leftover crisp can be stored in an airtight container for up to 4 days—although it is best enjoyed warm on the day you make it!

Note † WE LIKE TO QUICKLY BLITZ HALF OF THE OATS IN A FOOD PROCESSOR UNTIL THEY ARE MORE FINELY GROUND, CREATING MORE TEXTURE IN THE CRISP TOPPING. THIS IS COMPLETELY OPTIONAL, THOUGH!

Banana "Nice" Cream, Two Ways

We always keep frozen banana slices on hand so that we can whip up a batch of this when a sweet tooth hits. Neither of us can have dairy-based ice cream, but we don't even miss it with this yummy alternative!

The consistency is more like soft serve, so if you prefer your ice cream harder, we recommend making it ahead of time and freezing for at least an hour before enjoying.

New-tella Nice Cream

Serves 2

1½ CUPS FROZEN BANANA CHUNKS (2 TO 3 BANANAS)

2 TABLESPOONS CHOCOLATE-HAZELNUT CASHEW BUTTER (PAGE 58)

TOASTED HAZELNUTS, FOR GARNISH

TOASTED CACAO NIBS, FOR GARNISH

1. In a food processor or blender, combine the frozen banana and the nut butter. Blend the mixture until incorporated, 1 to 2 minutes.
2. Divide between two bowls, and top with toasted hazelnuts and cacao nibs.
3. If the banana cream will not be served immediately, transfer to the freezer to store for up to 3 days.

GLUTEN-FREE + DAIRY-FREE + VEGAN + REFINED SUGAR-FREE + PALEO

Mint Chocolate Chip Nice Cream

Serves 1

1 CUP FROZEN BANANA CHUNKS (1 TO 2 BANANAS)

2 TABLESPOONS CLASSIC SMOOTH NUT BUTTER (PAGE 62)

DASH OF PEPPERMINT EXTRACT

2 TABLESPOONS CHOCOLATE CHIPS

1. In a food processor or blender, combine the frozen banana, nut butter, and peppermint extract. Blend the mixture until incorporated, 1 to 2 minutes.
2. Add the chocolate chips and blend for an additional 20 to 30 seconds so that chunks of chocolate chips remain but get broken up a bit.
3. Transfer the mixture to a bowl. Serve immediately, or place bowl in the freezer and store for up to 3 days.

GLUTEN-FREE + DAIRY-FREE + VEGAN

Chocolate "Caramel" Crunch Bars

Makes 36 (3/4 by 2-inch) bars

Once on Halloween, Julie dressed up as a "nut butter witch." She wore one of our Ground Up aprons and a witch's hat, and handed out small jars of nut butter from the pockets of her apron. As you can see, being the "nut butter ladies" has really taken a hold of our identities.

But if everyone was handing out Halloween treats that were good for you, wouldn't the world be just a little bit of a better place? (If only for the sake of children's sugar highs!)

It got us thinking about how we could replicate the traditional candy bar with good-for-you ingredients, and we remembered how much dates and nut butter mixed together tastes remarkably like caramel. This recipe for healthy candy bars may take a bit of extra effort, we realize, but the results are so worth it. And since one batch yields thirty-six bars, it's an easy recipe for sharing.

¾ CUP SHREDDED UNSWEETENED COCONUT, TOASTED

⅓ CUP CACAO NIBS, TOASTED

¼ CUP COCONUT FLOUR

¼ TEASPOON VANILLA EXTRACT, OR SEEDS FROM ¼ VANILLA BEAN

⅛ CUP BROWN RICE SYRUP (MOLASSES OR AGAVE SYRUP WOULD ALSO WORK)

½ CUP MAPLE SYRUP, DIVIDED

1¼ TEASPOONS SEA SALT, DIVIDED

1¼ CUP PITTED MEDJOOL DATES, ABOUT 35

1 CUP PLUS 2 TABLESPOONS COCONUT OIL, DIVIDED, PLUS EXTRA FOR GREASING PAN

1 CUP CLASSIC SMOOTH NUT BUTTER (PAGE 62), DIVIDED

1 CUP UNSALTED CHOPPED CASHEWS, TOASTED (OR "CRUNCH" OF CHOICE)

1⅓ CUP UNSWEETENED DUTCH-PROCESSED COCOA POWDER

INSTANT ESPRESSO POWDER, TO BLEND INTO THE CARAMEL OR CHOCOLATE (OPTIONAL)

ADDITIONAL CACAO NIBS, COCONUT FLAKES, OR TOASTED CASHEWS, FOR FINISHING (OPTIONAL)

(CONTINUED)

GLUTEN-FREE + DAIRY-FREE + VEGAN + REFINED SUGAR-FREE

1. Preheat the oven to 350°F. Grease an 8 by 8-inch cake pan with coconut oil.
2. Make the base layer in a medium-size bowl. Mix together the shredded coconut, cacao nibs, coconut flour, vanilla, brown rice syrup, ¼ cup of the maple syrup, and ¼ teaspoon of the sea salt.
3. Using a spatula, transfer the mixture to the prepared pan, and bake for 12 to 14 minutes, or until golden brown. Remove from the oven and refrigerate for at least 20 minutes.
4. Make the caramel layer in a food processor. Process the dates and 2 tablespoons of the coconut oil until a smooth paste is formed, approximately 2 minutes. Add in ⅓ cup of the nut butter and ¼ teaspoon of the sea salt and process an additional 1 to 2 minutes, or until smooth.
5. Remove the base layer from the refrigerator. Use a wooden spoon or spatula to evenly spread out the remaining ⅔ cup of nut butter over the base layer. Transfer to the freezer and let sit for at least 15 minutes.
6. Remove the base layer from the freezer. Use a wooden spoon or spatula to evenly spread out the caramel mixture over the nut butter layer, then top with the toasted cashews, pressing the cashews into the caramel using a piece of parchment paper or a plate. Place the pan in the freezer and let sit for at least 3 hours.
7. Make the chocolate in a medium saucepan. Melt the remaining 1 cup of coconut oil over low heat. Whisk in the remaining ¼ cup of maple syrup, the cocoa powder, the remaining ¾ teaspoon of sea salt, and the espresso powder if using. Keep the chocolate mixture warm over low heat.

8. Line a baking sheet with parchment paper. Remove the cake pan from the freezer and transfer the cake to a cutting board. Cut the cake into ¾ by 2-inch rectangles to get thirty-six bars total.
9. Use tongs to carefully dip each square into the saucepan and coat in the chocolate mixture. Transfer to the parchment paper–lined baking sheet. Continue dipping the bars in the chocolate mixture until all of them have been coated. Sprinkle the bars with your topping of choice.
10. Transfer the baking sheet to the refrigerator. When the chocolate has hardened, about 30 minutes, transfer the bars to an airtight container and store in the refrigerator, where the bars will keep for up to 1 month. These are best enjoyed straight from the refrigerator; if they thaw for too long, the bars lose their crunch.

Note † WE LIKE WRAPPING A COUPLE UP IN A CUTE GIFT BAG AND GIFTING TO FRIENDS AROUND THE HOLIDAYS.

Chocolate + Jam Thumbprints

Makes 12 cookies

Every Fourth of July, Julie's family goes berry picking and then spends the day canning their own raspberry jam. This salty and sweet recipe is the perfect way to pair her homemade jams with our nut butters. These chocolate–almond butter thumbprints are dotted with cacao nibs and toasted hazelnuts, then filled with tart homemade jam.

1 CUP CHOCOLATE-HAZELNUT CASHEW BUTTER (PAGE 58)

6 TABLESPOONS MAPLE SYRUP

6 TABLESPOONS OAT FLOUR

¾ TEASPOON SEA SALT

2 TABLESPOONS CACAO NIBS, TOASTED (OPTIONAL)

2 TABLESPOONS TOASTED HAZELNUTS, COARSELY CHOPPED (OPTIONAL)

¼ CUP RASPBERRY JAM

1. In a medium bowl, combine the nut butter, maple syrup, oat flour, and sea salt until incorporated. Fold in the cacao nibs and toasted hazelnuts if using.
2. Cover the bowl, and transfer the mixture to the refrigerator for at least 2 hours.
3. Preheat the oven to 350°F. Line a baking sheet with parchment paper.
4. Roll the dough into 1-inch balls. Place them about 2 inches apart on the baking sheet, and flatten.
5. Make an indent in the center of each with your thumb, then fill each hole with 1 teaspoon of jam.
6. Bake for 10 to 12 minutes, or until the outsides of the cookies are firm but not dark or crispy.
7. Let the cookies cool for 10 to 15 minutes before serving, or transfer to an airtight container to store for up to 5 days.

GLUTEN-FREE + DAIRY-FREE + VEGAN

Turkish Coffee Chocolate Chip Cookies

Makes 16 to 18 cookies

If you've ever enjoyed a Turkish coffee, you know just how delicious and powerful the flavors of cardamom and espresso are together. The strongly brewed coffee is beautifully complemented by the warmth and brightness of ground cardamom, and it's traditionally served in a small silver mug. Here, we bring those flavors to life in a gooey chocolate chip cookie, using our Cardamom Almond-Cashew Butter. We like the crunch of cacao nibs paired with the gooey chocolate chips, but feel free to omit one or the other. Our Ground Up Espresso Stout Nut Butter (page 50) would also work here; simply add 2 teaspoons of ground cardamom and omit the espresso powder.

1 EGG

1 TEASPOON VANILLA EXTRACT, OR SEEDS FROM 1 VANILLA BEAN

1 CUP CARDAMOM ALMOND-CASHEW BUTTER (PAGE 47)

¼ CUP MAPLE SYRUP

½ CUP COCONUT SUGAR

1½ TABLESPOONS INSTANT ESPRESSO POWDER

1 TEASPOON BAKING SODA

⅓ CUP ALMOND FLOUR

2 TABLESPOONS COLLAGEN PEPTIDES, UNFLAVORED (PAGE 177)

½ CUP VEGAN CHOCOLATE CHIPS

½ CUP CACAO NIBS, TOASTED

FLAKY SEA SALT, FOR FINISHING

GLUTEN-FREE + DAIRY-FREE

1. Preheat the oven to 350°F. Line a baking sheet with parchment paper.
2. In a large mixing bowl, combine the egg, vanilla, nut butter, maple syrup, coconut sugar, espresso powder, baking soda, almond flour, and collagen peptides. Mix until fully incorporated; the batter will be very sticky.
3. Fold in the chocolate chips and cacao nibs.
4. Place the dough in the refrigerator to chill for at least 2 hours.
5. Remove from the refrigerator and drop 1-tablespoon dollops onto the parchment-lined pan, about 3 inches apart. The cookies will spread out considerably, so the spacing is important.
6. Sprinkle each cookie with a pinch of flaky sea salt.
7. Bake the cookies for 7 to 9 minutes, or until the edges have darkened and become crispy and the tops are puffy.
8. Let the cookies cool for 10 to 15 minutes before serving; this is important because the cookies will fall apart if you try to move them before they're ready. Transfer the cookies to an airtight container to store for up to 5 days.

Snickerdoodle Swirl Skillet Cookie

Makes 1 (9-inch) skillet cookie

Inspired by the mighty PBJ sandwich, we created this skillet cookie to mimic our favorite childhood combo. We had a lot of trouble naming this creation—it's a cookie, a cake, and a blondie all in one. It could be served at brunch, as a dessert, or as an afternoon snack with tea or coffee. The base is a moist, cinnamon-spiced cookie cake, which is then swirled with jam for a stunning and tart contrast.

When we served it to friends, they were shocked to learn it wasn't loaded with flour and sugar. They loved the flavors, especially the cinnamon and coconut. This is also delicious if you omit the jam and add chocolate chips instead.

¼ CUP COCONUT OIL, MELTED, PLUS EXTRA TO GREASE THE PAN

2 EGGS

½ TEASPOON ALMOND EXTRACT

1 TEASPOON VANILLA EXTRACT, OR SEEDS FROM 1 VANILLA BEAN

1 CUP CINNAMON SNICKERDOODLE NUT BUTTER (PAGE 54)

½ CUP COCONUT SUGAR

1 TEASPOON BAKING SODA

½ TEASPOON BAKING POWDER

¼ TEASPOON SEA SALT

½ CUP ALMOND FLOUR

¼ CUP JAM OF CHOICE (WE PREFER MARIONBERRY)

FINE SEA SALT, TO FINISH

(CONTINUED)

GLUTEN-FREE + DAIRY-FREE

1. Preheat the oven to 325°F. Grease a 9-inch cast-iron skillet with coconut oil.
2. In a large bowl, combine the eggs, almond extract, vanilla, nut butter, the ¼ cup of coconut oil, and the coconut sugar. Mix to incorporate.
3. Add the baking soda, baking powder, the ¼ teaspoon of sea salt, and the almond flour. Mix again to incorporate.
4. Transfer the dough to the skillet and, using a spatula, evenly spread to the edges.
5. Top with the jam, and use a butter knife to swirl the jam into the batter in a circular motion. Sprinkle with the fine sea salt.
6. Bake for 28 to 30 minutes, or until the top is golden brown and the edges just start to fold in.
7. Slice into wedges to serve. Store slices in an airtight container for up to 5 days.

Almond Layer Cake with Cardamom Frosting + Cacao Nibs

Makes 1 (9-inch) cake

If you *really* love your best friend, this is the cake you'll make them on their birthday. Honey-sweetened and gluten-free, this cake is the mystical unicorn of all cakes. It's so moist, rich, and flavorful that you wonder how it could possibly be real. (Real, as in, really actually healthy and made with real ingredients.)

The shining star of this recipe is the coconut milk and cardamom nut butter frosting. Adding nut butter to frosting is easily one of our favorite flavor "hacks." We often just swap out the butter in a standard frosting recipe for nut butter, and it makes it instantly more flavorful (and conveniently dairy-free).

This cake is composed of two layers: a light cardamom-spiced almond layer and a rich dark-chocolate and orange layer. If two layers feels ambitious, feel free to make only one—it will still be delicious; just note that you won't need as much frosting. The coconut milk for the frosting needs to be chilled in the refrigerator for at least 8 hours or overnight before using so that it separates. You will only use the heavy cream part on the top.

Tips +

THE KEY TO A LIGHT AND FLUFFY CAKE LIES IN PROPERLY BEATING THE EGG WHITES. TO DO SO, MAKE SURE THAT ABSOLUTELY NO YOLKS GET MIXED IN WITH THE WHITES, AND KEEP THE BEATERS AND THE BOWL YOU'RE MIXING THEM IN AS CLEAN AS POSSIBLE. IN ADDITION, BEAT THE EGG WHITES ON MEDIUM SPEED, AND STOP AS SOON AS YOU'VE ACHIEVED STIFF PEAKS. (IF YOU BEAT THEM FOR MUCH LONGER, THE CAKE WILL BE LESS LIGHT AND TENDER.)

YOU COULD MAKE BOTH CAKES AT THE SAME TIME AND BAKE THEM TOGETHER, BUT WE PREFER TO MAKE ONE LAYER AND THEN THE NEXT, SO THAT'S HOW THE RECIPE IS WRITTEN.

(CONTINUED)

GLUTEN-FREE + DAIRY-FREE + REFINED SUGAR-FREE + PALEO

ALMOND CAKE

COCONUT OIL, FOR GREASING PANS

4 EGGS

1 TEASPOON FRESHLY SQUEEZED ORANGE JUICE

2 TEASPOONS ALMOND EXTRACT

1 TEASPOON SEA SALT

½ TEASPOON BAKING SODA

½ CUP HONEY

1¾ CUPS ALMOND FLOUR

1 TEASPOON GROUND CARDAMOM

CHOCOLATE-ORANGE CAKE

4 EGGS

1 TABLESPOON FRESHLY SQUEEZED ORANGE JUICE

2 TEASPOONS VANILLA EXTRACT, OR SEEDS FROM 2 VANILLA BEANS

1 TEASPOON SEA SALT

½ TEASPOON BAKING SODA

FINELY GRATED ZEST OF ½ ORANGE

½ CUP HONEY

1½ CUPS ALMOND FLOUR

½ CUP UNSWEETENED NATURAL COCOA POWDER

CARDAMOM NUT BUTTER FROSTING

2 13.5-OUNCE CANS COCONUT MILK, CHILLED

¼ TEASPOON SEA SALT

1 CUP CARDAMOM ALMOND-CASHEW BUTTER (PAGE 47)

½ CUP HONEY

1 TEASPOON VANILLA EXTRACT, OR SEEDS FROM 1 VANILLA BEAN

GARNISH

⅓ CUP CACAO NIBS, TOASTED, PLUS EXTRA FOR GARNISH

CANDIED ORANGE, FOR GARNISH

SLIVERED ALMONDS, TOASTED, FOR GARNISH

1. To make the almond cake: Preheat the oven to 350°F. Lightly grease two (9-inch) cake pans with the coconut oil.
2. Set out two large mixing bowls. Separate the eggs, dividing all the egg whites into one bowl and the egg yolks in the other. In the first bowl, use an electric mixer to mix the egg whites on high speed for 1 minute, until foamy. Add the orange juice, then beat at medium speed for 3 to 5 minutes, until stiff peaks form. (Be careful not to overbeat.) Set aside.
3. In the second bowl, mix the egg yolks, almond extract, sea salt, baking soda, and honey until fully incorporated, around 2 minutes. Mix in the almond flour and cardamom until incorporated, around 1 minute.
4. Gently fold in one-third of the egg white mixture, then incorporate the remaining two-thirds slowly and gradually, being sure not to lose the aeration. The batter will be light and airy and pale yellow in color. Using a spatula, transfer the batter to a greased cake pan.
5. Bake the cake for 14 to 16 minutes, or until the top is golden brown and firm to the touch. (To test, jiggle the pan a bit; there should not be any movement on the top.)
6. To make the chocolate cake: Use two large mixing bowls to separate the eggs, dividing all of the egg whites in one bowl and the egg yolks in the other. In the first bowl, use an electric mixer to mix the egg whites on high speed for 1 minute, until foamy. Add the orange juice, then beat at medium speed for 3 to 5 minutes, until stiff peaks form. (Be careful not to overbeat.) Set aside.
7. In the second bowl, mix the egg yolks, vanilla, sea salt, baking soda, orange zest, and honey until fully incorporated, around 4 minutes. Mix in the almond flour and cocoa powder until incorporated, around 1 minute.

(CONTINUED)

8. Gently fold in one-third of the egg white mixture, then incorporate the remaining two-thirds slowly and gradually, being sure not to lose the aeration. The batter will be light and airy but a bit denser than the almond cake batter. Transfer the batter to a greased cake pan.

9. Bake the cake for 13 to 15 minutes, or until the top is firm to the touch. (To test, jiggle the pan a bit; there should not be any movement on the top.) Let both cakes cool for at least 1 hour before frosting.

10. To make the frosting: The coconut milk separates when it's chilled, so a thick layer of white cream sits at the top of the can. Scoop out the cream part of the milk, measuring out 1½ cups. (Reserve any remaining liquid in the cans for another use; it's great for adding to smoothies, oatmeal, and soup.) Use an electric mixer to beat the coconut cream with the sea salt, nut butter, honey, and vanilla. Cover the bowl with plastic wrap, and transfer to the freezer for at least 1 hour to chill and thicken. (This can be made the night before and kept in the refrigerator overnight.)

11. To assemble the cake, carefully remove the cake layers from their pans. Using a serrated knife, thinly slice the rounded top off the almond layer to form an even surface for frosting, then place the almond layer on a cake stand or plate. Using an offset spatula, cover the top with half of the frosting, and sprinkle with the ⅓ cup of cacao nibs.

12. Place the chocolate cake on top, then proceed to frost the entire cake with the remaining frosting. Garnish the cake with cacao nibs, candied orange, and slivered almonds. Serve immediately, or transfer to the refrigerator before serving; the cake will keep for up to 5 days. (This cake should not sit out at room temperature for more than a couple of hours or the frosting will melt.)

Chocolate-Espresso Nut Butter Cups

Makes 12 cups

OK, we admit it, we are raging chocoholics, if you haven't already figured that out. We always keep cacao close by during long workdays for that caffeine boost! Since most chocolates are sweetened with cane sugar and often have added dairy, we started making these honey-sweetened nut butter cups for a quick fix. Not only are they incredibly easy to make (only four ingredients) but also they are sugar-free, Paleo, and seriously tasty.

Any nut butter would be delicious with these, but our favorite is the Ground Up Espresso Stout for its mocha flavor. You can get creative with toppings, as well; we love the crunch from the added cacao nibs, but you could also add dried fruit or toasted nuts on top.

If you don't have a muffin pan, don't fret! We've also made these using a 9 by 13-inch loaf pan. Simply swirl dollops of nut butter throughout, and cut them into bars. You could also use a mini muffin pan for bite-size treats!

1½ CUPS COCONUT OIL

2 CUPS UNSWEETENED DUTCH-PROCESSED COCOA POWDER

⅓ CUP HONEY OR MAPLE SYRUP

½ TEASPOON VANILLA EXTRACT, OR SEEDS FROM ½ VANILLA BEAN

¾ TEASPOON SEA SALT, PLUS ADDITIONAL FOR SPRINKLING

5 TABLESPOONS ESPRESSO STOUT NUT BUTTER (PAGE 50) OR NUT BUTTER OF CHOICE

CACAO NIBS, TOASTED, FOR SPRINKLING

1. Line a 12-cup muffin pan with paper cupcake liners.
2. In a small saucepan over medium heat, gently melt the coconut oil until all of the chunks dissolve.
3. Stir in the cocoa powder and gently mix until melted and no clumps remain.
4. Whisk in the honey, vanilla, and sea salt until smooth.

(CONTINUED)

GLUTEN-FREE + DAIRY-FREE + VEGAN OPTION + REFINED SUGAR-FREE + PALEO

5. Fill each muffin cup with enough of the warm cocoa mixture to cover the bottom by approximately ¼ inch.
6. Place the pan in the freezer for 10 minutes, or until the bottom has hardened. In the meantime, keep the remaining cocoa mixture warm on the stovetop over low heat.
7. Remove the pan from the freezer, and place about 1 teaspoon of the nut butter in each liner.
8. Drizzle the remaining warm cocoa mixture on top of each chocolate–nut butter cup, dividing evenly.
9. Top with a sprinkle of sea salt and the cacao nibs.
10. Place the cups in the freezer and let harden for at least 1 hour.
11. Remove from the freezer and serve. Store in the freezer or refrigerator for up to 3 months; cups may melt if they are left out at room temperature.

Grilled Peaches with Ice Cream + Snickerdoodle Drizzle

Serves 6

We love to host barbecues in the summer, and this is most often the dessert we serve when we do. While the guests are still enjoying dinner, we toss a few peaches on the grill. By the time we're done with the main dish, the peaches are tender, juicy, and sweet . . . dessert is ready! We add a scoop of ice cream and a hefty drizzle of nut butter, and we've got more-than-happy guests.

For an autumnal spin, replace the peaches with pears and opt for baking instead of grilling.

3 RIPE PEACHES, HALVED AND PITTED

2 TABLESPOONS EXTRA-VIRGIN OLIVE OIL

2 CUPS DAIRY-FREE VANILLA ICE CREAM

6 TABLESPOONS CINNAMON SNICKERDOODLE NUT BUTTER (PAGE 54), WARMED

1. Preheat a gas grill to medium heat. (If using a charcoal grill, wait until the fire has died down but the coals are still hot.)
2. Brush the cut sides of the peaches with the olive oil.
3. Place the peach halves on the grill, cut side down. Cook for 4 to 5 minutes, until grill marks appear.
4. Turn the halves over, and move them to indirect heat (or lower the heat). Cook for 10 to 12 minutes, or until the peaches are juicy and tender but not too mushy.
5. Top each peach half with a scoop of the ice cream and a drizzle of the nut butter.
6. Serve the dessert while the peaches are still warm and the ice cream is cold.

GLUTEN-FREE + DAIRY-FREE + VEGAN

No-Bake Hazelnut–Chai Oatmeal Cookies

Makes 18 cookies

These no-bake cookies could not be easier or more flavorful thanks to our sweet and salty nut butter. Like so many of our recipes, this is a super-versatile base recipe consisting primarily of oats, nut butter, and honey, so feel free to get creative. In this version, we've blended the delicious spices of a warm chai latte with our Ground Up Oregon Hazelnut Butter.

2 CUPS OLD-FASHIONED ROLLED OATS

1 CUP OREGON HAZELNUT BUTTER (PAGE 56)

⅓ CUP HONEY

½ TEASPOON SEA SALT

1 TEASPOON GROUND CINNAMON

½ TEASPOON GROUND CARDAMOM

½ TEASPOON GROUND NUTMEG

¼ TEASPOON GROUND CLOVE

2 TABLESPOONS CACAO NIBS, TOASTED, FOR GARNISH

2 TABLESPOONS CANDIED GINGER, CHOPPED, FOR GARNISH

1. To make the dough in a food processor: Quickly pulse the oats so that about half of them are broken up into smaller pieces. Add in the nut butter, honey, sea salt, cinnamon, cardamom, nutmeg, and clove. Process until just incorporated and a doughy texture forms, approximately 1 minute.

   Alternatively, to make the dough by hand: Heat the nut butter and honey together in a small saucepan on low heat, and mix together until both are melted and fully incorporated. Transfer to a large bowl and gently fold in the oats, spices, and sea salt until a dough texture forms, approximately 1 to 2 minutes.

2. Line a baking sheet or plate with waxed paper.

GLUTEN-FREE + DAIRY-FREE + VEGAN OPTION + REFINED SUGAR-FREE

3. Drop 1½-tablespoon dollops onto the baking sheet. Sprinkle a few cacao nibs and candied ginger pieces over each cookie. Use a fork to flatten the tops.
4. Place the cookies in the freezer for 15 minutes to harden. Transfer to the refrigerator and store cold for up to 1 month.
5. Remove the cookies from the refrigerator when ready to serve. These will soften quite a bit at room temperature. If the cookies will be sitting out for a while, store them in the freezer beforehand.

Sweet Citrus Salad with Honey-Mint Dressing

Makes 2 to 3 servings

We know what you're thinking. Salad as a dessert? That's crazy talk! What's actually crazy is how simple to prepare yet full of flavor this recipe is. Get ready to impress your guests and stay true to healthy choices, even in your desserts. Carolyn first started making this salad when she struggled to find a sweet treat to bring to a friend's house that fit her dietary constraints.

Although this makes for a refreshing summer dessert, it's best enjoyed during the winter when citrus season is at its peak. We recommend using Cara Cara or blood oranges.

2 ORANGES, PEELED AND THINLY SLICED

¼ CUP HONEY-MINT DRESSING (PAGE 106)

HANDFUL COARSELY CHOPPED FRESH MINT, FOR GARNISH

⅛ CUP TOASTED COCONUT FLAKES, FOR GARNISH

TEASPOON BEE POLLEN (OPTIONAL)

1. Arrange the orange slices on a plate.
2. Drizzle the oranges with the dressing. Garnish with the chopped mint, toasted coconut, and bee pollen if using. Serve immediately.

GLUTEN-FREE + DAIRY-FREE + VEGAN + REFINED SUGAR-FREE + PALEO

CHAPTER NINE:

Stacking the Pantry

We recognize that some of the ingredients in this cookbook may be new to you, so we wanted to provide some background on what we recommend keeping on hand, and what we look for when we're shopping for these products ourselves.

Most of these ingredients are best stored in glass jars or containers in cool, dark places. If you're looking for more information about buying and storing nuts and seeds, see the Guide to Nuts + Nut Butters (page 17).

Oils + Vinegars

We primarily use two oils in this cookbook: coconut oil and olive oil. On occasion we use ghee, or clarified butter, since it is better for those with dairy sensitivities. Please note that you can substitute butter for ghee in any recipe.

COCONUT OIL

Coconut oil is an excellent all-purpose oil due to its tolerance for high heat. We like to use it for everything from roasting vegetables to frying eggs to baking cookies.

Rich in saturated fats, coconut oil is typically solid at room temperature. We recommend storing your jar near the stovetop to keep it warmer and semi-solid if you live in a cooler climate like us. You'll notice that in recipes where we use coconut oil, we indicate that it should be melted beforehand, which can either be done on the stovetop or in a microwave.

Coconut oil is a great dairy-free replacement for butter in baked goods, with a subtly sweet flavor. (Coconut oil does not actually have a strong coconut taste.) Its high fat content is also known to promote healthy brain development and contribute to strong bones.

When choosing coconut oil, always look for **virgin** and **unrefined**, to ensure that it has not been overly processed and still retains healthy nutrients and flavor.

OLIVE OIL

We use olive oil primarily as a finishing oil, best in salad dressings and sauces. Rich in antioxidants and vitamin E, olive oil is great for the liver and gallbladder, as well as for heart health.

When shopping for olive oil, choose bottles that are labeled **"extra-virgin"** and **"unrefined."** Be sure to check the ingredients on your bottle, as well, since many brands on the market will actually mix genetically modified canola oil in with olive oil.

COCONUT AMINOS

Coconut aminos is made from the sap of coconut blossoms, which is blended with salt and naturally aged. It makes a great substitute for soy sauce because it's soy-free and gluten-free, and it is also

Paleo Diet–friendly. We love adding it to dressings, sauces, and marinades for a rich and salty flavor, such as in our Cardamom Satay Sauce (page 109).

You can purchase coconut aminos in many grocery stores now (you'll usually find it by the soy sauce), as well as online.

Natural Sweeteners

When we say "natural sweeteners," we mean sugars that occur naturally in foods such as fruit and those that haven't been overly processed. Refining a natural sugar, such as cane sugar, means stripping it of its naturally occurring minerals and fiber and oftentimes chemically treating or bleaching it. We prefer to focus on more natural sweeteners that are lower on the glycemic index, meaning they have less of a spike on blood sugar.

HONEY

Honey is one of nature's greatest wonders, in our opinion. Full of enzymes, nutrients, and antioxidants, honey is naturally healing and can even be effective as an antibacterial agent.

Always choose **raw, unpasteurized** honey, so that it retains its antimicrobial powers. If you can buy honey from a local beekeeper, even better.

MAPLE SYRUP

Like honey, maple syrup is a naturally occurring liquid sweetener. It also takes, on average, 40 gallons of maple sap to yield 1 gallon of maple syrup. We use it in small quantities, just enough to impart sweetness.

Maple syrup is divided into two grades—Grade A and Grade B. While Grade A is lighter and more delicate, Grade B has a more distinct and rich maple taste. The latter is best for when you want to impart maple flavor in nut butters and desserts.

In most of the recipes in this cookbook, you can substitute maple syrup for honey; just keep in mind that we find it to be slightly sweeter than the former.

You want to make sure to purchase **pure maple syrup**, as some brands will dilute theirs with high fructose corn syrup.

COCONUT SUGAR

Touted for its lower glycemic index, coconut sugar is collected from the sap of coconut palms, which is distilled down and dried out. (It is also called "coconut palm sugar" or "coconut nectar.") It is the closest substitution for cane sugar in baked goods, though distinctly less sweet. It adds a toasty richness to recipes, most closely comparable to brown sugar.

It contains trace minerals and nutrients from the coconut palm, including iron, zinc, calcium, and potassium. We try not to use coconut sugar abundantly, but it is the best alternative for many baked goods recipes—and it is also Paleo Diet–friendly. When buying coconut sugar, try to choose brands that are committed to sustainable harvesting and environmentally friendly practices. If you don't have coconut sugar on hand or would like a more affordable alternative, try substituting raw turbinado sugar—it is the least refined cane sugar option.

DATES + DRIED FRUITS

Mineral-rich and full of fiber, we love to use dates as a natural sweetener, enjoyed both on their own (Stuffed Dates, Two Ways, page 97) and in treats (Cinnamon–Date Chia Bars, page 90). Always select dried fruits with **no added sugar or oils**. When choosing dates, we always opt for **pitted Medjool dates**—they are plumper and sweeter, and the pits are already removed!

Grains

OATS

All of the recipes with oats in this cookbook call for old-fashioned rolled oats. While oats are naturally gluten-free, many are processed on the same machinery as wheat, so be sure to choose those that are certified gluten-free if you are allergic to gluten.

OAT FLOUR

Oat flour is made from simply grinding up oats, making it easy to whip up a batch of oat flour in your home food processor. Simply add oats and grind them up until they are a fine, flour-like texture.

We like to use oat flour as a cheaper alternative to other gluten-free flours—it is especially nice for Chocolate + Jam Thumbprints (page 152).

COCONUT FLOUR

Coconut flour is made from finely ground dehydrated coconut meat. We love it because it's a great alternative for baking when you're on a restricted diet.

When baking with coconut flour, note that it is highly absorbent. You will need only ⅓ cup of coconut flour to replace 1 cup of regular flour in a recipe—but you will also need to increase the amount of eggs or liquid. We like it in recipes such as Coconut Crêpes with Chocolate-Hazlenut Cashew Butter (page 70).

ALMOND FLOUR

Almond flour, also called "almond meal," is made from finely ground almonds. You can make your own at home using a food processor to grind up almonds until they turn into a fine flour. However, you have to be careful not to overprocess or else it will turn into nut butter. In our experience, we have found it's safer and easier to just buy almond meal at the store rather than make it on our own.

Superfoods + Additives

SALT

If you're wondering what that extra zip you're missing in your nut butters is, there is a good chance it's sea salt. Not only is salt a flavor enhancer but also it is a natural preservative, and it actually helps to extend the shelf life of nut butters. In addition, salt aids blood sugar control by improving insulin sensitivity, which helps to balance out any spikes from the natural sugars in honey or nuts.

We tend to be a little salt-obsessed; in fact, Carolyn has an entire collection of fancy sea salts in her pantry. We tried not to go overboard with the amount of salt in any of these recipes, so feel free to adjust the salt quantities to your taste.

When buying salt, choose a good quality, unrefined, kosher sea salt, which is known to contain valuable trace minerals including potassium, iron, and zinc.

VANILLA

We are committed to using whole, unprocessed vanilla beans in our nut butters, and one of our favorite tasks in the kitchen is scraping the fresh vanilla seeds from their bean pods.

Vanilla bean is quite expensive, and when you are not flavoring large batches like we are, vanilla extract may make more sense. We include options for both in our recipes—and if you're ever unsure, the ratio is 1 vanilla bean to 1 teaspoon of vanilla extract.

When buying vanilla, look for either plain vanilla beans, vanilla bean paste without additives, or a high-quality vanilla extract. (We don't recommend vanilla powder, since the first ingredient on the ingredient list is sugar.)

CHOCOLATE + COCOA POWDER

Always choose 100 percent pure unsweetened cocoa powder. There are two types of cocoa powder: natural and Dutch-processed. Natural cocoa powder is untreated, making it more acidic and therefore sharper in taste. (It is also more common.) Dutch-processed cocoa powder goes through an alkalization process to remove some of the cocoa's natural acidity, making it darker in color yet milder and more bittersweet in taste. The main difference in baking with them is your choice of leavening agent; use baking soda with natural cocoa, and use baking powder with Dutch-processed cocoa. We use natural cocoa powder in baked goods, such as our Fudgy Walnut Brownies (page 142), and Dutch-processed in confections, such as our Chocolate "Caramel" Crunch Bars (page 149).

When selecting chocolate or chocolate chips, opt for the darkest you can find, and ideally with no added milk or dairy. Regardless of what you choose, nearly all chocolate chips have a small percentage of refined sugar, so we make a small exception in some recipes to include those.

CACAO NIBS

Cacao nibs are chocolate in its most unrefined form—the seeds of the cacao tree, shelled and broken down into small pieces. Cacao nibs are essentially what the process of making chocolate starts with. Filled with antioxidants, minerals, and healthy fat, they are also mildly stimulating since they contain theobromine (which is comparable to caffeine). Quite bitter in taste, we love to add them to sweeter desserts to bring balance and texture. We use these in a lot of our recipes, but feel free to omit or replace with sweetened chocolate chips.

We almost always toast our cacao nibs before using them, as it makes their taste milder and less bitter. To toast cacao nibs, evenly distribute them on a baking sheet and bake for 5 to 10 minutes at 350°F. You'll know they're done when they are fragrant and slightly darker in color.

It can be hard to find cacao nibs in grocery stores, particularly for a reasonable price, so we recommend purchasing them online in bulk. Always choose raw and organic.

CHIA SEEDS

As an excellent source of omega-3 fatty acids, chia seeds are a wonderful superfood to add to recipes and to nut butters. They are also rich in antioxidants and provide fiber, iron, and calcium. They are the star ingredient in our Mocha Chia Pudding Parfait (page 75), and when they are incorporated into other recipes. When chia seeds are added to a liquid, they will retain that moisture, becoming plump and gelatinous.

COLLAGEN PEPTIDES

Collagen, an incredible protein-rich nutrient derived from bovines, is known for its ability to promote gut health, skin and hair strength, joint health, and more. While bone broths and gelatin also provide a collagen boost, collagen peptides have become an increasingly popular form. Collagen peptides are a hydrolyzed form of collagen, so they come in a neutral-tasting powder that can be easily added to smoothies, water, baked goods, and more. Haven't baked with collagen peptides before? These healthy amino acids not only add a nutritional boost to baked goods, such as our Turkish Coffee Chocolate Chip Cookies (page 154) but also they absorb some of the moisture, helping to retain structure in grain-free desserts.

We prefer unflavored collagen peptides, which you can find in many grocery stores or purchase through online retailers.

NUTRITIONAL YEAST

Most vegans should be well-acquainted with nutritional yeast. This deactivated form of yeast not only is replete with B vitamins but also lends a remarkably "cheesy" quality to dairy-free sauces and dishes. We use it in our Creamy Vegan “Alfredo” Sauce (page 108), but it is also great sprinkled atop grain bowls, scrambled eggs, and more.

You can find nutritional yeast in flake or powder form (we prefer flakes) in the bulk section of most health food stores and grocery stores.

Nut Butters

If you’re interested in making the recipes in this cookbook but don’t have the time to make your own nut butters, don’t fret. We won’t judge if you buy your nut butters. (In fact, we recommend Ground Up! All of our nut butters are free of added sugars and oils, and we have a number of unique flavors to choose from. You can order online at *grounduppdx.com*.)

When shopping for nut butters, pay attention to the ingredient list. You’d be surprised how many brands add filler ingredients. Avoid any that have added oil (especially palm oil or other hydrogenated oils), ingredients you aren’t familiar with (what the heck do “natural flavors” mean anyway?), and refined sugars, including cane sugar and agave.

Acknowledgments

We are so grateful to our community for helping this book come to life.

To our customers—thank you for supporting our business, genuinely caring about our success, cheering us on through the trials and tribulations of starting and running a small business, and, finally, for sharing with us all of the ways you use our nut butter (many of which have turned into recipes in this book). Your creativity and ingenuity inspire us.

To our friends and loved ones, we couldn't have done this without your help. You lent us an ear when we needed to talk through a recipe idea, a mouth when we needed a taste tester, and a supportive hug in those moments when it all just felt like too much.

We are especially grateful to our recipe testers, who eagerly tried out these recipes in their home kitchens—when all we could offer was nut butter and our deepest gratitude in return. We are particularly grateful to our mothers, Sally and Connie, for their hilarious commentary in providing feedback, on all matters, and loving support when we needed it.

We also want to give a huge thank-you to the team at Andrews McMeel Publishing, without whom this book wouldn't have been possible. To our editor, Jean Lucas, for taking a chance on us and guiding us through this process; to our designer, Diane Marsh; and to our production editor, Elizabeth Garcia.

We want to express our immense gratitude to our literary agent, Joy Tutela, at The David Black Literary Agency. You nurtured our vision and pushed us to bring it to life, even if it felt scary and we fought imposter syndrome and we didn't feel like we were ready. We are so glad this cookbook dream became a reality.

Finally, we want to thank our Ground Up team—the women who picked up our slack while we holed up to write this book, who cheered us on and tasted recipes and kept things running smoothly during a busy holiday season. You motivate us to be better managers, business owners, and individuals. We dedicate this cookbook to you.

GROUND UP
- PDX -

HEALTH BENEFITS

PEANUT-FREE

1. Peanuts aren't nuts! Technically, they're legumes (and they grow underground).
2. Peanuts often contain high levels of aflatoxin, a carcinogen linked to liver cancer and kidney cancer, which is produced by a fungus in soil where peanuts are typically grown.
3. Approx. 0.6-1.3% of the US population is allergic to peanuts. (Compare that with 0.4-0.6% to tree nuts.)
4. We believe food diversity is important and want to make it easier to incorporate other nuts into your diet!

HONEY-SWEETENED

1. Less processed than other sweeteners, it's naturally occuring and produced locally!
2. Honey acts as a natural preservative and is antimicrobial, making our nut butters last even longer!
3. A little goes a long way! Each 12-ounce jar of our nut butter contains less than 1 tablespoon of honey.
4. Honey is the only acceptable sweetener on the SCD and GAPS diets because it is easier to digest and absorb.

We use grade A Pacific Northwest clover honey.

WHY YOU SHOULD AVOID CANE SUGAR

Sugar is not only highly processed but it is "empty calories"—without any nutrients or health benefits. In fact, mounting evidence shows that consuming large amounts of table sugar can lead to chronic inflammation, liver toxicity, and disease.
(Source: NutritionFacts.org)

NO ADDED OILS!

95% of commercial nut butters contain added oils. This is most often used as a filler to make their product cheaper. It is NOT necessary to make nut butter. (When you grind nuts, they release their own natural oils!)

ALMONDS + CASHEWS

1. Excellent sources of magnesium—great for muscle cramps, immune function, and more.
2. Contain high amounts of calcium—providing bone strength and more.
3. Great source of protein—at 5 grams per serving—especially for vegans and vegetarians.

SALT SALT SALT

Salt gets a bad rap, but we couldn't imagine our nut butters without it!
1. Salt acts as a natural preservative, helping to extend the shelf life of our products.
2. It aids blood sugar control by improving insulin sensitivity, which helps to balance out any spikes from the natural sugars in honey or nuts.
3. Salt contains valuable minerals, including potassium, iron, and zinc.

We use an unrefined, mineral-rich sea salt from Jacobsen Salt Co.

HEART-HEALTHY

Our nut butters are full of heart-healthy fats, including omega-3 and omega-6!

ALMOND BUTTER VS PEANUT BUTTER

50% Less Saturated Fat	7x More Calcium
3x More Vitamin E	2x More Fiber
2x More Iron	2x More Magnesium

DAIRY-FREE GLUTEN-FREE SOY-FREE PEANUT-FREE SUGAR-FREE

groundupPDX.com | @groundupPDX | hello@groundupPDX.com

Metric Conversions + Equivalents

METRIC CONVERSION FORMULAS

To Convert	Multiply
Ounces to grams	Ounces by 28.35
Pounds to kilograms	Pounds by .454
Teaspoons to milliliters	Teaspoons by 4.93
Tablespoons to milliliters	Tablespoons by 14.79
Fluid ounces to milliliters	Fluid ounces by 29.57
Cups to milliliters	Cups by 240
Cups to liters	Cups by .236
Pints to liters	Pints by .473
Quarts to liters	Quarts by .946
Gallons to liters	Gallons by 3.785
Inches to centimeters	Inches by 2.54

APPROXIMATE METRIC EQUIVALENTS

Weight

¼ ounce	7 grams
½ ounce	14 grams
¾ ounce	21 grams
1 ounce	28 grams
1¼ ounces	35 grams
1½ ounces	42.5 grams
1⅔ ounces	47 grams
2 ounces	57 grams
3 ounces	85 grams
4 ounces (¼ pound)	113 grams
5 ounces	142 grams
6 ounces	170 grams
7 ounces	198 grams
8 ounces (½ pound)	227 grams
16 ounces (1 pound)	454 grams
35.25 ounces (2.2 pounds)	1 kilogram

Length

⅛ inch	3 millimeters	2½ inches	6.25 centimeters
¼ inch	6.25 millimeters	4 inches	10 centimeters
½ inch	1.25 centimeters	5 inches	12.75 centimeters
1 inch	2.5 centimeters	6 inches	15.25 centimeters
2 inches	5 centimeters	12 inches (1 foot)	30.5 centimeters

Volume

¼ teaspoon	1 milliliter	½ cup (4 fluid ounces)	120 milliliters
½ teaspoon	2.5 milliliters	⅔ cup	160 milliliters
¾ teaspoon	4 milliliters	¾ cup	180 milliliters
1 teaspoon	5 milliliters	1 cup (8 fluid ounces)	240 milliliters
1¼ teaspoon	6 milliliters	1¼ cups	300 milliliters
1½ teaspoon	7.5 milliliters	1½ cups (12 fluid ounces)	360 milliliters
1¾ teaspoon	8.5 milliliters	1⅔ cups	400 milliliters
2 teaspoons	10 milliliters	2 cups (1 pint)	480 milliliters
1 tablespoon (½ fluid ounce)	15 milliliters	3 cups	720 milliliters
2 tablespoons (1 fluid ounce)	30 milliliters	4 cups (1 quart)	0.96 liter
¼ cup	60 milliliters	1 quart plus ¼ cup	1 liter
⅓ cup	80 milliliters	4 quarts (1 gallon)	3.8 liters

COMMON INGREDIENTS AND THEIR APPROXIMATE EQUIVALENTS

1 cup uncooked white rice = 185 grams

1 cup all-purpose flour = 120 grams

1 stick butter (4 ounces • ½ cup • 8 tablespoons) = 110 grams

1 cup butter (8 ounces • 2 sticks • 16 tablespoons) = 220 grams

1 cup brown sugar, firmly packed = 213 grams

1 cup granulated sugar = 200 grams

OVEN TEMPERATURES

To convert Fahrenheit to Celsius, subtract 32 from Fahrenheit, multiply the result by 5, then divide by 9.

Description	Fahrenheit	Celsius	British Gas Mark
Very cool	200°	95°	0
Very cool	225°	110°	¼
Very cool	250°	120°	½
Cool	275°	135°	1
Cool	300°	150°	2
Warm	325°	165°	3
Moderate	350°	175°	4
Moderately hot	375°	190°	5
Fairly hot	400°	200°	6
Hot	425°	220°	7
Very hot	450°	230°	8
Very hot	475°	245°	9

Information compiled from a variety of sources, including *Recipes into Type* by Joan Whitman and Dolores Simon (Newton, MA: Biscuit Books, 1993); *The New Food Lover's Companion* by Sharon Tyler Herbst (Hauppauge, NY: Barron's, 2013); and *Rosemary Brown's Big Kitchen Instruction Book* (Kansas City, MO: Andrews McMeel, 1998).

Index

D

E

F

G

Nut Butter

Andrews McMeel Publishing
a division of Andrews McMeel Universal
1130 Walnut Street, Kansas City, Missouri 64106

www.andrewsmcmeel.com

groundauppdx.com

19 20 21 22 23 TEN 10 9 8 7 6 5 4 3 2 1

ISBN: 978-1-4494-9948-8

Library of Congress Control Number: 2019932743

Editor: Jean Z. Lucas
Art Director/Designer: Diane Marsh
Production Editor: Elizabeth A. Garcia
Production Manager: Carol Coe